creative living

ROWAN

creative living

Thirty two projects by Gail Abbott and Jane Bolsover

Photography by **Mark Scott**

A ROWAN PRODUCTION

First published in Great Britain in 2003 by Rowan Yarns
Green Lane Mill, Holmfirth
West Yorkshire, England HD9 2DX

Location manager and Styling: **Gail Abbott**
Photography: **Mark Scott**
Book and Jacket design: **Downes Design**
Illustrations: **Carolyn Jenkins**
Technical illustrations: **Siriol Clarry**
Sub editor: **Natalie Minnis**

British Library Cataloguing-in-Publication Data.
Rowan Yarns
Creative Living
ISBN 1-904485-00-6

Colour reproduction by Chroma Graphics (Overseas) Pte. Ltd
Printed and Bound in Singapore by KHL Printing Co. Pte. Ltd

The publishers have made every effort to ensure that all instructions
given in this book are accurate, but cannot accept liability for any
resulting loss or damage, whether direct or consequential and
howsoever arising.

About the Photographer
Mark Scott is a location lifestyle photographer specializing in Interiors,
gardens and travel. His relaxed style and fresh lighting has earned him
commissions for numerous UK publications and his work regularly
appears in magazines such as *Woman & Home*, *Ideal Home* and
House Beautiful.

introduction

We were both highly delighted with the response to Rowan Living last year, the first book for which we joined forces to design 30 ideas for the home using the Kaffe Fassett Fabric Collection. Reviews and extracts appeared in many mainstream interiors and crafts magazines, and everyone seemed to be just as enthusiastic about making accessories for the home in these fabrics as we are.

For this our second book we set off for the wide-open spaces of the North Norfolk coastline with curtains, bedlinen and cushions and bags brimming over with all the other makes, to stay in a beautiful barn conversion that sits right on the edge of the salt marsh. The cry of the curlews woke us each morning, and we were able to stand on the balcony to watch the gleam of the sky reflected in the narrow creeks as the tide came creeping up twice a day, or witness spectacular sunsets without moving from the upstairs living room. The light along this coastline is wonderful at midsummer, and photographer Mark Scott made the most of it. I hope you'll agree that the photographs make it so much harder to decide which projects to make; they all look so gorgeous.

We both feel inspired by everything we see around us, from the colours seen along the side of a painted beach hut, or the spicy hues of paprika and saffron, to the primary shades of a scattering of children's wooden beads. Even the simple shapes of a piece of cake cut for afternoon tea can spark off an idea. Each section of this book begins with a page of inspirational shots to give you an idea of where we got our ideas from, and to help you get your own creative juices flowing.

There are bedroom ideas using stripy fabrics in seaside blues and greens, blowsy floral designs for summer living rooms and a kaleidoscope of adorable spotty colour for a child's nursery. Rich Madras checks in spice colours have been sewn into practical and charming beach accessories, and the chalky pastels of the Shot Cotton range coordinate easily together for a teatime treat. Decide on your own favourites or mix and match the colours to create a personal slant on our ideas. Whatever projects you choose we hope you love sewing them as much as we did.

seaside stripes

Painted beach huts blistered by the sun, marram grass whispering in the ocean breeze gently stinging bare legs as you walk down to the beach for buckets of shells. Then a slow stroll back to the pier for seaside candy, a stripy deckchair to sit on and watch sailing boats scudding over the waves. These are the things that make up our summer holiday memories. Be inspired by the seaside and reach for striped fabrics in aquamarine, blue and sea green. Whether you're at home or on holiday, you'll feel you're on the beach when you stitch up a collection of easy makes for your bedroom and bathroom.

appliqué bedlinen & oxford cushion

Fresh and pretty for summer, dress up your bed with these delightful
little sailing boats appliquéd to a plain white sheet on a sea of narrow
stripes. Make simple matching pillowcases, and an Oxford cushion
bordered with two rows of contrasting satin stitch.

appliqué bedlinen

YOU WILL NEED

Boat-edged sheet – ■ 90cm (1yd) of 114cm- (45in-) wide Rowan Stripe (RS 02) ■ 30cm (⅓yd) 114cm- (45in-) wide Lime (SC 43) Shot Cotton ■ Small piece of Jade (SC 41) Shot Cotton ■ Small piece of Pachrangi Stripe (PS 01) ■ Paper-backed fusible web ■ Matching thread ■ Contrast coloured stranded embroidery thread ■ Single sheet ■ Appliqué templates on page 106

Matching pillowcase – ■ 1m (1¼yds) of 114cm- (45in-) wide Rowan Stripe (RS 02) ■ Matching thread

TO MAKE

Boat-edged sheet

1 For the turn-back, cut two strips of Rowan Stripe fabric the width of the fabric by 35cm (13¾in) and join the strips to make one long length. Trim seam turnings and press seam open. Trim length of strip to width of the sheet, allowing for a 1.5cm (⅝in) seam allowance at each end.

2 Iron the fusible web on to the wrong side of the Jade Shot Cotton, Pachrangi Stripe and remaining Rowan Stripe. Using the boat appliqué templates trace off five boat hulls and flags on to Pachrangi Stripe, five large sails on to the Rowan Stripe and five small ones on to the Shot Cotton. Cut out all the pieces.

3 Cut the Lime Shot Cotton into five equal pieces 23 x 26cm

(9 x 10¼in). Peel the paper backings off the appliqué pieces and arrange them onto each Lime piece. Press pieces in place using a hot iron.

4 Set your sewing machine to a medium-sized, close zigzag stitch, and using toning thread, stitch around the edges of the appliqué pieces, enclosing all the raw edges. Continue stitching down the straight side of the large sail to the hull to form the mast. Press edges of appliquéd patches 1.5cm (⅝in) to wrong side.

5 Press the edges of the striped turn-back strip 1.5cm (⅝in) to wrong side. Lay sheet out flat with right side uppermost and lay strip on top, right side up, lining one long edge up with the stitchline on the deep hemmed end of the sheet, usually 5cm (2in) in from one end. Baste and stitch the strip in place keeping side edges level and working close to the edge.

6 Arrange the five appliquéd pieces on to the striped strip placing the outer ones about 5cm (2in) in from the sides and the others spaced equally in between. Baste edges in place. To stitch patches permanently in place, thread a needle with a length of stranded embroidery thread and work a row of small evenly spaced running stitches 3mm (⅛in) in from the edges. Remove all basting stitches.

Matching pillowcase

1 With the stripes running along the long edges, cut one rectangle 51 x 98cm (20 x 38½in) and one 51x 83cm (20 x 32⅝in). At one short end of the larger rectangle press a double-turned 1.5cm (⅝in) hem to the wrong side and stitch in place. At short end of the of the smaller rectangle press over a 1.5cm (⅝in) hem to the

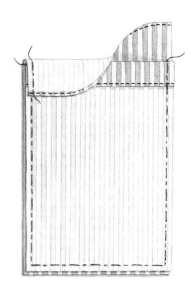

wrong side and then press over a further 5cm (2in) and stitch in place.

2 With right sides facing, place the smaller rectangle on top of the larger one, with short raw ends and side edges level. Baste the two rectangles together around the raw outer edges. Fold the exposed part of the larger rectangle down over the hemmed edge of the smaller rectangle (see diagram) and baste the folded over section in place along the side edges. Machine pillowcase pieces together around the three raw edges with a 1.5cm (⅝in) seam allowance. Neaten turnings together, turn pillowcase through to right side and press flat.

oxford cushion

YOU WILL NEED
■ 70cm (¾yd) of 114cm- (45in-) wide Rowan Stripe (RS 02)
■ 70cm (¾yd) of 114cm- (45in-) wide Jade (SC 41) Shot Cotton
■ 45cm (18in) square cushion pad ■ Two shades of thread to match the Rowan Stripe ■ Fade-away fabric marker pen

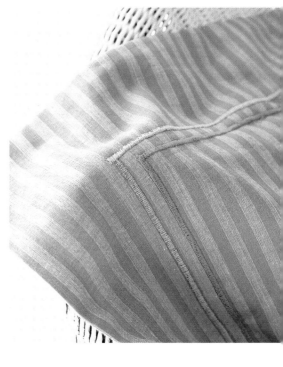

TO MAKE

1 From the Rowan Stripe cut one front cover 64cm (25in) square. From the Shot Cotton cut two back pieces 45 x 64cm (17¾ x 25in).

2 Press a 1.5cm (⅝in) hem to wrong side down one long edge of each back cover piece then press over a further 3cm (1¼in) to wrong side. Machine stitch in place close to first pressed edge.

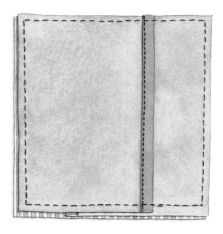

3 Lay the front cover right side uppermost on a flat surface and place the back covers face down on top, raw edges level and hemmed edges overlapping at the centre.

4 Baste the cover pieces together around all sides. Machine stitch around all four sides with a 1.5cm (⅝in) seam allowance. Trim seam turnings, clip corners, remove basting stitches and turn to right side. Push out corners well and press seamed edges flat.

5 Working on the right side of the front cover and using the fade-away marker pen, draw a border 7cm (2¾in) in from each side edge. Set your sewing machine to a medium-sized, close zigzag stitch, and using the lighter shade of thread, stitch around the borderline. Change to the darker thread and work a second borderline 1cm (⅜in) inside the first. Press work and insert cushion pad through the back opening.

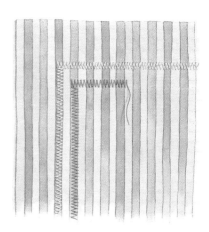

padded hangers & lavender shoe fresheners

Bring the scent of summer into your bedroom with these softly padded
hangers made with dried lavender. They are ideal for delicate clothing and
will help keep the inside of the wardrobe fresh – or make our simple
little lavender sachets to keep shoes and slippers sweetly smelling too.

padded hangers

YOU WILL NEED

■ Fabric to cover hanger (see step 4 for quantity).
We used Rowan Stripe (RS 02), Jade (SC 41) and Lime (SC 43) Shot Cottons
■ Medium weight 4oz polyester batting (see step 1 for quantity)
■ 30cm (⅓yd) of 12mm- (½in-) wide matching Shot Cotton or Rowan Stripe
bias binding – see 'Making bias binding' in the Technique know-how, on
page 89 ■ Wooden coathanger ■ Dried lavender heads (optional)
■ 50cm (20in) of narrow satin ribbon for bow
■ Matching thread

TO MAKE

1 Measure the length of the coathanger, then wrap a tape measure around it to find out its overall width. Cut out a piece of batting the length of the hanger plus 1cm (⅜in), by the overall width of the hanger plus 3cm (1¼in)

2 Fold the batting in half lengthways and pierce a small hole in the centre of the folded edge. Slip the coathanger hook through the hole in the batting. Smooth the batting around the hanger, overlapping the two long edges. Pin the edges together inserting some dried lavender heads as you go. Hand sew all the edges of the batting together with large herringbone stitches (see Technique know-how, page 92), enclosing the lavender heads.

3 Cover the coathanger hook by wrapping the bias binding around it, securing ends in place with a few small hand stitches.

4 Measure the overall width of the padded hanger. Cut out a piece of fabric one and a half times the length of the hanger by the overall width of the padded hanger plus 2cm (¾in).

5 Press the two long edges of the fabric 1cm (⅜in) to the wrong side. Fold the fabric in half length-ways, right sides together, and

machine stitch across the short ends with a 1cm (⅜in) seam allowance. Turn to right side.

6 Place the hanger inside the fabric with the hook at the centre. Starting at the base of the hook and finishing at one end of the hanger, bring the two pressed edges together with small running stitches (see Technique know-how, page 92), leaving end of thread hanging and inserting more lavender as you go. Repeat, sewing a second line of stitches from base of hook to remaining end of hanger. Pull up both sets of gathers evenly and secure threads.

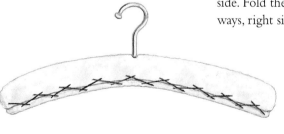

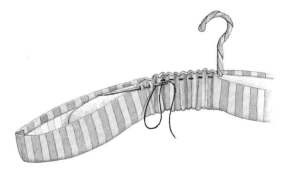

DID YOU KNOW?

Placing lavender heads inside your hangers will help to ward off moths and bugs, while scenting your clothes at the same time.

7 Tie the ribbon into a bow around base of hook. Replenish scent at intervals with a few drops of essential oil.

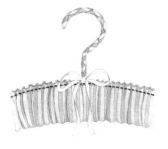

To make two-tone hanger
Follow steps 1, 2 and 3 above, then measure for the main fabric cover as shown in step 4 allowing for a strip one and a half times the length of the hanger. Divide the length measurement for the strip into four, and cut two end pieces to a quarter of the length by the calculated width, and one centre section to half of the length by the width, adding a 1.5cm (⅝in) seam to all edges. Seam the pieces together into one long strip and continue to cover hanger following steps 5, 6 and 7 above.

lavender shoe fresheners

YOU WILL NEED
■ 30cm (½yd) of 114cm- (45in-) wide Broad Stripe (BS 23)
■ Dried lavender heads to fill
■ Matching thread
■ 50cm (20in) of Russia braid
■ Template on page 107

TO MAKE

1 Using the template, cut two shapes to fold of fabric. With right sides together, pin and stitch around the curved edge, leaving the top edge open. Clip curved seam turnings; turn to right side and press.

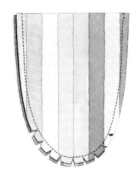

2 Turn under and press a double turned hem along the raw top edge. Stitch in place and press. Fill 'bag' with lavender and tie tightly around the top with the Russia braid. Repeat steps 1 and 2 for second shoe freshener.

CREATIVE TIP

When you need to revive your shoe freshener's fragrance, simply untie the braid bows and sprinkle in some drops of lavender essential oil.

toiletries bag, shower cap & trimmed towels

A medley of stripes combine to make a gorgeous set of bathroom accessories. The circular toiletries bag has a fresh, minty blue lining and the elasticated shower cap is bound around the edge with the same fabric. Nothing could be easier than trimming a set of white towels with strips of fabric that are zigzag-stitched in place.

toiletries bag

YOU WILL NEED

■ 70cm (¾yd) of 114cm- (45in-) wide Pachrangi Stripe (PS 01)
■ 70cm (¾yd) of 114cm- (45in-) wide Jade (SC 41) Shot Cotton
■ 15cm (6in) diameter circle of card
■ 2.5cm (1in) square of lightweight iron-on interfacing
■ Matching thread ■ Chalk marker pencil
■ 60cm (24in) of matching Russia braid or fine satin ribbon
■ Drawing pin and a length of string

TO MAKE

1 From both the Pachrangi Stripe and Shot Cotton cut out a 61cm (24in) diameter circle. On the striped circle measure 6cm (2⅜in) and 7.5cm (3in) in from the edge at one point. Mark positions with dots of chalk pencil and join dots together with a line. Press the interfacing square to the wrong side of the fabric under the chalk line and work a small buttonhole at the position marked.

2 Fold the plain Shot Cotton circle into quarters to find the centre and mark the position with a pin. With right sides facing, stitch the two circles together with a 1cm (⅜in) seam allowance, leaving a 15cm (6in) opening. Snip into the curved seam turnings and turn

through to right side. Carefully press seamed edges flat making sure seam lies right on the edge and press opening edges 1cm (⅜in) to the wrong side.

3 With the Shot Cotton side uppermost and using the chalk pencil attached to a length of string, draw a 15cm (6in) diameter circle from the marked central point. Remove pin. Slip the cardboard circle through the opening between the two layers of fabric and position it under the drawn circle. Baste card circle in place by stitching around the chalk line. Using a zipper foot on your machine, stitch the card circle permanently in place and remove the basting stitches.

4 Slipstitch opening edges together (see Technique know-how, page 91). Working on the Shot Cotton side, draw two circles, one 6cm (2⅜in) in from the edge and the other 1.5cm (⅝in) inside this. Machine stitch along the two chalked circles to form the draw cord channel. The buttonhole that you made at the beginning should sit between the two rows of stitching. Brush away any remaining chalk that still shows.

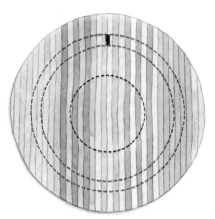

5 Using a bodkin or small safely pin, thread the Russia braid, or ribbon, through the buttonhole and around the channel. Knot the two ends together and pull to gather up the sides into the bag shape.

shower cap

■ 53cm (21in) of 114cm- (45in-) wide Broad Stripe (BS 23)
■ 53cm (21in) square of white P.V.C
■ 1.7m (2yds) of 2.5cm- (1in-) wide bias binding in Jade (SC 41)
Shot Cotton, see 'Making bias binding' in the Technique know-how,
on page 89 ■ Matching thread ■ Shirring elastic
■ Chalk marker pencil

TO MAKE

1 From both the Broad Stripe and P.V.C fabric cut out a 52cm (20½in) diameter circle. Lay the two pieces on top of each other with raw edges level and baste them together close to the edge.

2 Finish off the edges of the fabric with bias binding, folded in half lengthways with turnings inside and machine stitched over the raw edges, enclosing the basting. For a neat finish to the bias binding, press the ends 1cm (⅜in) to the wrong side and butt them up close together.

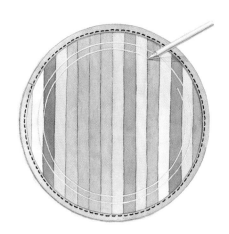

3 Using the chalk marker pencil, lightly draw a circle onto the fabric side of the hat 5cm (2in) in from the edge. Then draw a second one 1cm (⅜in) inside this. Work two rows of elasticised shirring around the chalk lines (see Technique know-how, page 90) to gather up the cap. Knot the ends of the elastic together on inside to prevent it from coming undone. Brush away any chalk marks that still remain on the right side of the cap.

---

trimmed towels

■ White towel
■ Two 7.5cm- (3in-) wide vertical strips of Narrow Stripe (NS 08) to fit width of towel plus 2cm (¾in)
■ Matching thread

TO MAKE

Press a 1cm (⅜in) hem to wrong side around all sides of each strip. Place strips onto towel about 7.5cm (3in) in from each end, covering the smooth braided sections at each end of towel. Baste in place keeping short ends level with sides of towel, then machine stitch around all edges using an open zigzag stitch. Remove basting stitches.

nursery spots

Summertime for a child is a kaleidescope of impressions – all the colours, sounds and smells that make up the endless sunny days. When choosing fabrics for a nursery, take your inspiration from the great outdoors and use a colour palette that reflects the blue of a summer sky or the green of a wild meadow. Think of the rainbow hues reflected in soap bubbles and mix them together in happy associations. Use zingy paint shades on the walls to stimulate creativity, co-ordinated bedlinen to encourage going to bed and make toys, a bed quilt and a pair of cotton pyjamas in spotty, dotty patterns.

bed quilt & seat pad

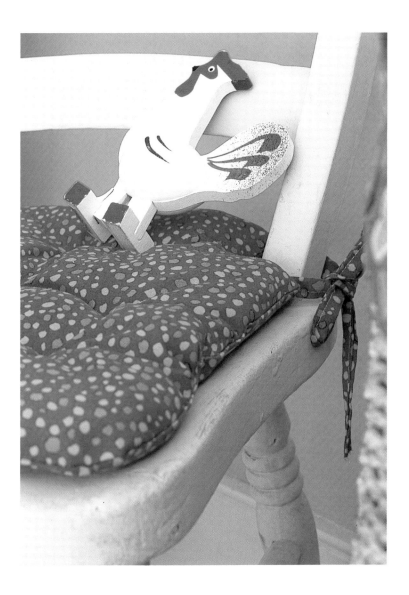

Put away continental quilts for the summer – our modern version of the traditional eiderdown is a cooler version for a child's bed when it's thrown over a sheet on warm nights. Next to the bed, a pint-sized wooden chair is made more comfortable with a jazzy tie-on seat pad.

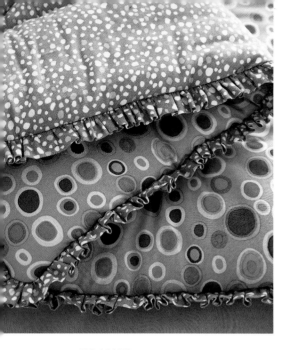

bed quilt

YOU WILL NEED

■ 2m (2¼yds) of 114cm- (45in-) wide Dotty in Lavender (GP 14-LV)
■ 1.6cm (1¾yds) of 114cm- (45in-) wide Bubbles in Sky Blue (GP 15-SB)
■ 4.8m (5¼yds) of 114cm- (45in-) wide 4oz polyester batting
■ Quilting diagram from page 105
■ Matching thread

TO MAKE

1 Cut a panel 114 x 153cm (45 x 60in) from both the Dotty and Bubbles fabrics and cut three panels the same size from the batting. From the remaining Dotty fabric cut six frill strips 6cm (2¾in) deep by the width of the fabric.

2 Lay the Bubbles panel face down on a flat surface and place the three batting panels on top, keeping raw edges level. Smooth gently until there are no wrinkles. Pin at the corners and midpoints of each side, close to the edges.

3 Beginning at the centre, baste diagonal lines outwards to the corners, making your stitches about 7.5cm (3in) long. Then, again starting at the centre, baste horizontal and vertical lines out to the edges.

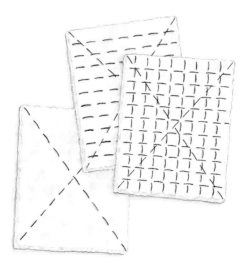

Continue basting until you have basted a grid of lines about 10cm (4in) apart over the entire quilt.

4 With right sides facing, join the short ends of the frill strips together to make one large circular ring. Press seams open and then with wrong sides together fold ring in half, bringing circular raw edges together. Press and baste raw edges together.

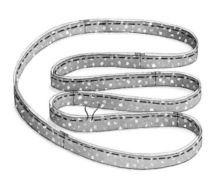

5 Work two rows of gathering stitches along the basted raw edges of each of the six strips of fabric that form the frill. Pull up gathers evenly to fit outer edge of quilt. Keeping raw edges level, pin and baste the frill to the right side of the quilt. Machine stitch in place with a 1cm (⅜in) seam allowance.

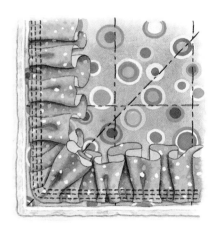

6 With right sides together, place the Dotty panel on top of the quilt, sandwiching the frill in between the layers. Baste and then machine stitch the layers together around the outer edge, with a 1cm (⅜in) seam allowance, leaving an opening along one edge for turning through.

7 Turn quilt to right side and slip stitch the opening edges together (see the Technique know-how section, page 91). Baste the Dotty side of the quilt to the batting following step 3.

8 Using the quilting diagram as a guide, mark out the quilting lines on the Dotty side of the quilt using a chalk pencil. Baste along each quilting line and then machine quilt the lines in place (see the Technique know-how section, page 91). When you've finished quilting, remove all the basting stitches.

seat pad

YOU WILL NEED

■ 50cm (½yd) of 114cm- (45in-) wide Dotty in Cobalt (GP 14-COB)
■ 1.2m (1⅓yds) of 25mm- (1in-) wide bias binding in Cobalt Dotty
(GP 14-COB), see 'Making bias binding' in the Technique know-how, on
page 89 ■ Matching thread ■ 50cm (½yd) of 90cm- (35in-) wide
thick polyester batting ■ Tracing paper

TO MAKE

1 To make a template, lay the sheet of tracing on the chair seat and trace around the edges. Add a 1.5cm (⅝in) seam allowance around all edges. Using the template cut one piece from batting and two pieces from fabric.

2 To make the ties, machine the pressed edges of the bias binding together, enclosing long raw edges. Cut the strip into two equal pieces. Place one of the cover pieces on the chair seat and mark positions where ties will attach to chair with pins. Fold each tie in half, bringing short raw ends together, and machine the folded ends securely to the right side of the cover piece at the positions marked.

3 With right sides facing, machine the two cover pieces together with a 1.5cm (⅝in) seam allowance, leaving a gap for turning through along the back edge. Trim seams and turn cover right side out. Trim 1.5cm (⅝in) away from all edges of batting, insert into cover and slipstitch gap closed (see the Techniques know-how section, page 91).

4 Tie the three layers of the seat pad together, at seven regularly spaced intervals. To do this, work a hand stitch through all the layers of fabric, pulling them up tightly and oversew the stitch several times to secure.

5 Neaten the raw tie ends by pushing them up inside the tie 'tubes'. Secure the pad to the chair by tying the ties in bows around the back uprights.

CREATIVE TIP

Save time by sewing on ready-made tapes or ribbons instead of making your own ties.

spotty pyjamas

Getting them ready for bed will never be a problem again with our
brightly spotted pyjamas. They're gorgeous in pink, but don't just make
them for the girls – with a buttoning jacket, breast pocket and elasticated
pants they will easily convert for boys too. To fit ages three to six.

spotty pyjamas

YOU WILL NEED
- 2.20m (2½yds) of 114cm- (45in-) wide Roman Glass in Pink (GP 01-PK)
- Large piece of paper ■ Scaled down pattern pieces page 100 & 101
- 30cm (⅓yd) of 90cm- (35½in-) wide lightweight iron-on interfacing
- Matching thread ■ Four 15mm (⅝in) buttons
- 70cm (27½in) of 32mm-(1¼in-) wide elastic

Note: A 1.5cm (⅝in) seam allowance is included throughout. Stitch seams with right sides together, unless otherwise instructed.

TO MAKE

Making the Jacket

1 Scale up the pyjama pattern pieces on to a large piece of paper, as indicated on pages 100 and 101. Using the full-sized pattern pieces cut two front shirts, one back shirt, two sleeves, two collars, one pocket and four legs.

2 Press interfacing to front shirts at positions marked on pattern. Neaten the pocket top edge, press 2.5cm (1in) to the wrong side and machine stitch in place. Press the remaining raw edges of pocket 1.5cm (⅝in) to wrong side. Baste, then machine stitch the side and bottom edges of pocket to one front shirt (left front for girls, right front for boys), matching top corners to dots on pattern.

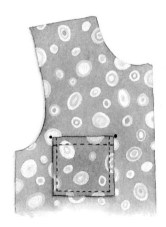

3 Machine the two front shirts to the back shirt at the shoulder seams. Machine sleeves to armhole edges matching notches and centre sleeve head notch to shoulder seams. Machine side and sleeve seams in one continuous line of stitching.

4 Press interfacing to wrong side of one collar. Machine collars right sides together along the straight edges and short ends. Trim seams, snip corners and turn to right side. Press flat. Topstitch around seamed edges of collar, working close to the edge. Baste collar to neckline with raw edges together and shoulder seams matching the collar notches.

5 Neaten the straight interfaced edges of the front shirts. Press 6mm (¼in) to wrong side and stitch in place. Fold the interfaced front sections onto the right side of the front shirts and machine stitch around neckline from one folded edge to the other. Trim seam

turnings and neaten collar and neckline edges together. Fold the interfaced sections to the inside and press in place along the foldline to form the front facings.

6 Neaten sleeve and hem edges, press 2cm (¾in) to the wrong side and machine stitch in place. Work four vertical buttonholes on right front shirt for girls and left front shirt for boys, placing them 12mm (½in) in from the front edge, with the top one 7.5cm (3in) down from neck edge and the others spaced equally below.

CREATIVE TIP

If you don't want to work buttonholes, then use popper fasteners, or sew-on Velcro disks to fasten the jacket front.

Making the Trousers

7 Seam trouser legs together in pairs at side and inside leg seams. With right sides together, place one leg inside the other. Matching seams and raw waist edges, stitch crotch seams from one waist edge to the other.

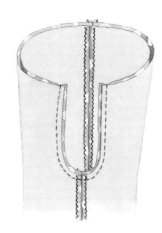

8 Neaten the waist edge and press 4cm (1½in) to wrong side. Machine around top edge close to fold and another line of stitching 3.5cm (1⅜in) below, leaving a gap at one side seam. Thread elastic through casing formed; adjust to fit waist. Stitch elastic ends together and trim surplus elastic. Machine gap closed. Neaten hem edges, press 2cm (¾in) to wrong side and then machine stitch in place.

31

jo jo the clown

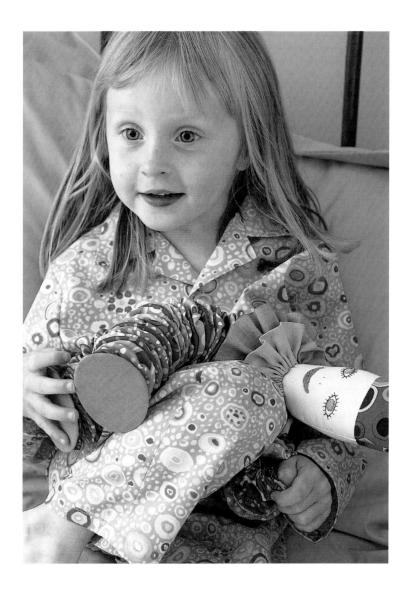

This jolly toy clown is sure to become a family favourite. Made from lots of different spotty fabrics, he's a great way to use up the smallest leftover scraps. Just gather up circles with running stitch and thread them onto strong elastic. He's so easy to make that you can ask the children to give you a hand.

jo jo the clown

YOU WILL NEED

■ 15cm (⅙yd) each of 114cm- (45in-) wide Water Melon (SC 33), Lime (SC 43) and Jade (SC41) Shot Cottons ■ 26cm (⅓yd) each of 114cm- (45in-) wide Dotty in Cobalt (GP 14-COB) and Lavender (GP 14-LV) ■ 26cm (⅓yd) each of 114cm- (45in-) wide Bubbles in Cobalt (GP 15-COB) and Sky Blue (GP 15-SB) ■ 26cm (⅓yd) each of 114cm- (45in-) wide Roman Glass in Pink (GP 01-PK) ■ 15cm (⅙yd) of 114cm- (45in-) wide calico fabric ■ Templates from pages 103 & 104 ■ Matching thread ■ Strong shirring elastic ■ Small piece of thin card ■ Polyester toy stuffing ■ Pink, blue and black stranded embroidery thread ■ Dressmakers' carbon paper

TO MAKE

1 Using the circular template, cut out a total of 62 circles from the different spotty fabrics. Thread a needle with a length of doubled thread and knot the end. Sew a running stitch around the outer edge of one circle, turning under a small hem to the wrong side as you work.

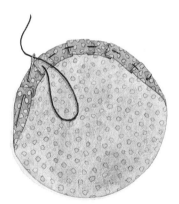

2 Gather up the running stitches, pulling the thread tightly. Secure with a small stitch and trim the end. Repeat with remaining circles.

3 Cut two feet from thin card and two foot covers from Water Melon Shot Cotton. Sew a running stitch around the edges of the feet as shown in step 1. Place a card foot in the centre of each and gather up running stitches, pulling tightly to enclose the card feet. Secure thread.

4 Cut out two face shapes from calico and two hat shapes from Cobalt Bubbles. Using the dressmakers' carbon paper, transfer the face details onto one face shape. With right sides together and using a 6mm (¼in) seam allowance, stitch a hat to a face shape along the straight edges. Press seams open.

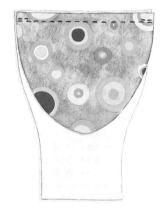

5 With right sides facing, stitch the two joined hat and face shapes together, with a 6mm (¼in) seam allowance, matching the hat seamlines. Clip into curved seam turnings and turn right side out. Stuff with toy filling.

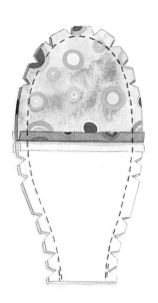

6 Cut four hand shapes from calico and stitch together in pairs around the curved edges. Clip curves, turn to right side and stuff with toy filling.

7 Cut one neck ruff from Lime Shot Cotton 9 x 56cm (3½ x 22in) and one from Jade Shot Cotton 12.5 x 56cm (5 x 22in). Fold each ruff in half across width, bringing short edges together and stitch down short edges to form two rings. Press seams open. Press a 6mm (¼in) hem to wrong side around each circular edge. With wrong sides together, fold ruffs in half bringing pressed edges together.

8 To form the legs, thread a large-eyed needle with a length of shirring elastic and firmly knot one end. Thread 12 of the gathered circles onto the elastic with gathered centres uppermost, picking up colours at random. Then, thread on another 12 with the gathered centres underneath. Knot off the elastic firmly.

9 To form body, thread a needle with elastic as before and thread on 18 circles with gathered centres underneath. Take the legs and separate the circles where you changed their direction (you should have 12 circles for each leg), wrap the needle and elastic from the body under the leg elastic and then thread it back up through the body to where you started. The legs should now be attached to the body. Fasten off the elastic securely.

10 Thread ten circles onto a length of elastic for an arm, with gathered centres uppermost. Take the needle between the two elastic threads under the top body circle and then thread on the remaining circles for the other arm. Fasten off securely.

11 Turn under the raw edges on the head and hands and hand stitch them in place. Hand stitch gathered feet to legs. Sew a running stitch around the pressed edges of each ruff and leave thread and needle still attached. Place the wider ruff over the head and gather up the running stitches, pulling the thread tightly. Secure with a small stitch and trim the end. Repeat with smaller ruff.

12 Using three strands of blue embroidery thread, backstitch around centres of eyes and fill in centres with satin stitch. Using one strand of black thread, blanket stitch in eyelashes. Using three strands of pink thread, chain stitch the mouth and make two small stitches for the nose (see Technique know-how, page 93 for stitch details).

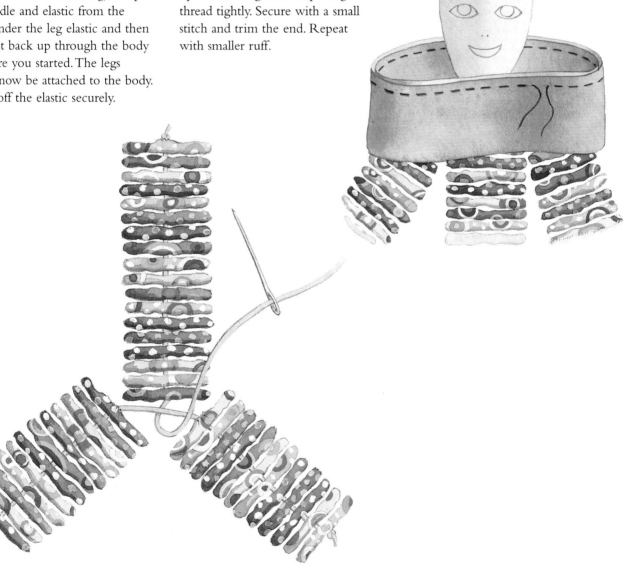

lined toy basket &
playful kite

Turn a wicker toy basket into a useful toy bin. The lining pulls out to become a drawstring bag for collecting up toys. Pop it back in the basket and hey presto, a tidy bedroom. For breezy summer days outdoors, choose a mix of spotted and plain fabrics for our bright kite. Let the children choose their own colours and help you make it up.

lined toy basket

YOU WILL NEED

■ 114cm- (45in-) wide Bubbles in Cobalt (GP 14-COB) and 114cm- (45in-) wide calico fabrics – see steps 1 and 2 to work out quantities ■ 23cm (¼yd) of 114cm- (45in-) wide Shot Cotton in Lime (SC 43) ■ Matching thread ■ Large circular laundry basket with lid ■ Large piece of paper

Note: A 1.5cm (5/8in) seam allowance is included throughout. Stitch seams with right sides together, unless otherwise instructed.

TO MAKE

1 To make a pattern for the base, measure the diameter of the basket base and divide it in half to find the radius. Using the radius measurement and a pencil attached to a length of string, draw a circle on the paper. Add a 1.5cm (⅝in) seam allowance all around the drawn circle and cut out along this line.

2 To work out the size of the side panel, measure the height of the basket and add 18cm (7in) for hems. Then, measure around the circumference of the inner circle on your base pattern and add 3cm (1¼in) for seam allowances. Cut out one side panel to these measurements and one circular base in both calico and Bubbles fabric.

3 With right sides together, fold the Bubbles side panel in half across its width, bringing short raw

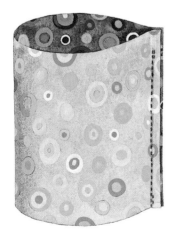

ends together. Stitch the short ends together to form a cylinder, starting 9cm (3½in) down from one edge to allow for an opening for the draw cord. Press seam open and opening edges 1.5cm (⅝in) to the wrong side.

4 Stitch the Bubbles base to the lower circular edge of the joined side panel, clipping into the side panel seam turnings to help you stitch a smooth curve. Repeat steps 3 and 4 with the calico pieces.

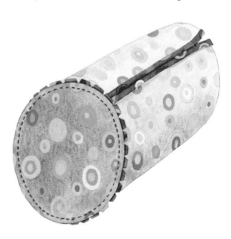

5 With wrong sides together, place the Bubbles liner inside the calico liner, matching up side seam and opening edges. Baste top raw edges together. Keeping pressed opening edges level, machine topstitch the layers together around the opening.

6 Press basted top circular edge 1.5cm (⅝in) to calico side and then another 4cm (1½in) to calico side. Machine stitch the lower pressed edge in place to form the draw cord channel.

7 For the draw cord, cut two strips of lime Shot Cotton across the width of the fabric, 9cm- (3½in-) wide. Trim off the selvedges and then join the two strips at one short end to form a long strip. Press seam open. With right sides together, fold strip in half along its length and stitch long edges together and across one short end. Clip corners and turn to right side, using a knitting needle or similar object to help push it through. Press seamed edges flat. Tuck in raw edges at remaining short end and slipstitch opening closed. Using a bodkin or large safety pin, thread the draw cord through the channel. Insert cover into basket and pull the top edge over onto right side of basket. Tie draw cord into a bow.

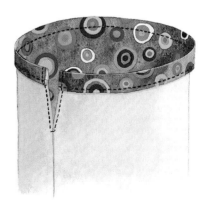

playful kite

YOU WILL NEED

■ 23cm (¼yd) of 114cm- (45in-) wide Dotty in Cobalt (GP 14-COB)
■ 23cm (¼yd) each of 114cm- (45in-) wide Jade (SC41) and Lime (SC 43) Shot Cottons ■ 23cm (¼yd) of 114cm- (45in-) wide Bubbles in Cobalt (GP 15-COB)
■ 2m (2⅛yds) of 2.5cm- (1in-) wide bias binding in Water Melon (SC 33) Shot Cotton – see 'Making bias binding' in the Technique know-how, on page 89
■ Scraps of Lavender (GP 14-LV) and Water Melon (SC 33) Shot Cottons
■ Templates from page 102 & 103 ■ Matching thread ■ 60cm (23½yds) of 46cm- (18in-) wide paper backed fusible web ■ 20m (22yds) of Roman blind cord ■ 20cm (8in) square of plastic coated fabric ■ Two 6mm (¼in) diameter eyelets ■ 1.2m (1½yds) of 6mm (¼in) wooden dowel
■ 20cm (8in) of 20 x 20mm (¾ x ¾in) timber ■ Pinking shears
■ Small piece of timber for a cord tidy

TO MAKE

1 Using the templates, cut out one top kite piece from both Cobalt Bubbles and Jade Shot Cotton, and one lower kite piece from both Cobalt Dotty and Lime Shot Cotton. Note: If you want your kite to have the right side of the print fabric on both sides, fuse two pieces of the print fabric wrong sides together, using the paper backed fusible web, before cutting out your pieces.

2 From the plastic-coated fabric cut two eyelet tabs, one base rod pocket, one top rod pocket and two side rod pockets, using pinking shears. For the tail bows cut two rectangles 6.5 x 15cm (2½ x 6in) from each of the cotton fabrics and fuse them together in matching pairs, using the paper-backed fusible web. Using the bow template and pinking shears cut out one bow from each piece of fused fabric.

3 Fold one of the eyelet tabs in half with the plastic coating outermost, and pin the raw edges to one of the top kite pieces at the position marked on template. Stitch the two top kite pieces together with a flat fell seam (see the Techniques know-how section, on

page 88), sandwiching the eyelet tab in between. Repeat with the remaining eyelet tab and the two lower kite pieces.

4 Stitch the top kite to the lower kite, with a flat fell seam, matching the centre seams. On the opposite side of the kite to the eyelet tabs, pin and stitch the base, top and side rod pockets to the points of the kite.

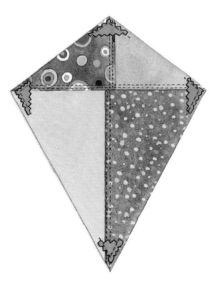

5 Finish the edges of the kite with the bias binding, folded in half lengthways with turnings inside and machine stitched over the raw edges, sandwiching the rod pockets between the binding. Take care not to stretch the outer edges of the kite as you attach the binding. For a neat finish to the binding, press ends 1cm (⅜in) to the wrong side and butt them up close together.

6 Thread a large-eyed needle with a 1.5m (60in) length of Roman blind cord and stitch it to the base point of the kite. Knot a tail bow to the cord, by winding it several times around the centre of the bow and securing in place. Space bows about 12cm (5in) apart.

7 Insert an eyelet into each eyelet tab and knot the end of the remaining Roman blind cord to one eyelet. Trim it to a length of approximately 20cm (8in). Knot the rest of the cord to the other eyelet and then knot the two cords together about 18cm (7in) along the longer length of cord. Tie the loose end of the cord around a small piece of timber and wind the cord around it.

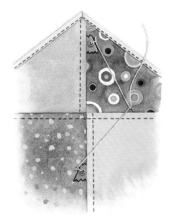

8 Cut the dowel into two lengths measuring 66cm (26in) and 52cm (20½in) long. Insert the dowels into the rod pockets – and your kite is now ready to fly.

spicy checks

The richness of oriental spices to tempt the senses: hot chilli peppers, aromatic cardamoms and mellow turmeric – all these give out their own special aroma, while their colours influence everything from ceramic tiles to woven cottons. Make the most of sultry summer weather with spicy shades woven into Madras checks and ginghams made up as a range of beach accessories. Deep-dyed pure cottons, hand loomed by weavers in India, are soft enough for a wrap-round sarong, yet strong enough for a sturdy windbreak when it's canvas-backed.

canvas windbreak & padded beach mat

The ultimate beach mat is made from quilted layers, with added jute ties.

It's perfect for sunbathing yet rolls up for carrying to and from the beach.

Enjoy the sunshine protected from sea breezes with our sturdy windbreak.

The removable canvas cover has bright checked borders.

canvas windbreak

YOU WILL NEED
- 2.3m (2½yds) of 114cm- (45in-) wide Broad Check (BC 04)
- 2.3m (2½yds) of 114cm- (45in-) cream cotton canvas
- Matching thread ■ Four windbreak poles (recycle old ones – alternatively, you could use four tapered broom handles)
- Four large headed tacks (optional)

TO MAKE

1 Cut out one rectangle of canvas 91 x 230cm (36 x 90in) and two strips of Broad Check 25.5 x 230cm (10 x 90in).

2 Press a 1.5cm (⅝in) hem to wrong side along one long edge of each checked strip. With right side of check to wrong side of canvas, stitch the remaining long raw edges of the checked strips to the long edges of the canvas piece.

3 Fold checked strips over on to the right side of the canvas and press seamed edges flat. Making sure check strips are lying flat and wrinkle free, pin and baste the loose pressed edges to the canvas. Topstitch the checked strips in place along both top and bottom edges.

4 Press a 1cm (⅜in) hem to wrong side along each short end of windbreak and then press over another 4.5cm (1¾in) hem and

machine stitch in place, to form the two outer pole channels.

5 Lay the windbreak out flat, wrong side up, and measure 70cm (27½in) along the top and bottom edges of the windbreak from one side pole channel row of machine stitching. Mark a row of pins to indicate position of next pole channel. Repeat, measuring from other end of the windbreak, for final pole channel. You should end up with two rows of pins parallel to the short ends.

6 Fold windbreak back along one row of pins so that right sides are together, keeping top and bottom edges level. Machine stitch another pole channel 4.5cm (1¾in) in from the pinned fold. Repeat to form the final pole channel along the remaining row of pins. Remove all pins and basting stitches. Push poles into channels. If desired, you can fasten the poles to the windbreak, by inserting a large headed tack through the back of each channel near the top of the windbreak.

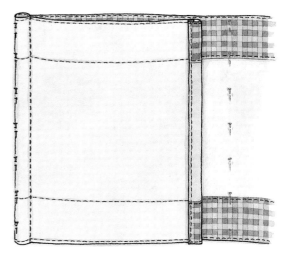

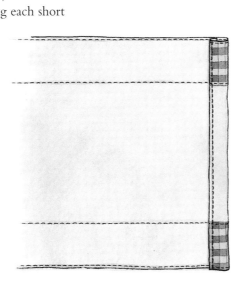

padded beach mat

YOU WILL NEED

■ 1.8m (2yds) of 114cm- (45in-) wide Exotic Check (EC 02)
■ 1.8m (2yds) of 114cm- (45in-) wide Tangerine (SC 11) Shot Cotton
■ 1.8m (2yds) of 90cm- (35½in-) wide medium weight
polyester batting ■ Fine jute string
■ Large-eyed needle ■ Matching thread

TO MAKE

1 From the checked fabric cut two rectangles, each 78 x 170cm (30¾ x 67in), and from the batting, one rectangle 75 x 167cm (29½ x 65¾in).

2 With right sides facing and raw edges level, stitch the two checked pieces together, leaving a long opening along one short edge. Clip corners and turn cover through to right side. Using a pointed object, poke out the corners well.

3 Carefully insert the batting through the opening, pushing it well down and into the corners. Smooth it out until it lies flat, then fold opening edges 1.5cm (⅝in) to wrong side and slipstitch edges together (see Technique know-how, page 91).

4 To tie the layers of the beach mat together, thread the needle with the fine jute string and make a small single stitch down through the layers from the right side of the mat and then back up again. Knot the ends of the string together a couple of times and cut off the excess leaving short ends about 1.5cm (⅝in) long.

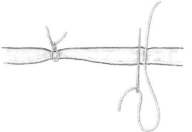

5 Work a row of these ties approximately 12cm (4¾in) in from each side edge of the mat and one row right down the centre, spacing each tie about 20cm (8in) apart down the length of the mat.

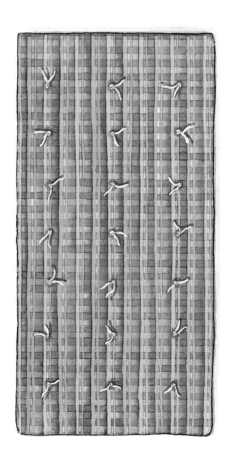

CREATIVE TIP

Want to make your mat waterproof for use on damp sand or grass?
Then cut the base panel from a plastic coated fabric and make it up in the same way.

lined picnic basket & summer sarong

Everyone loves a picnic but it's more of an occasion when you unpack it from a luxury hamper. We've chosen Narrow Check to make a padded lining to protect food while you carry it to the beach. Simply hem a square of fabric and use it as a tablecloth, a sarong skirt or sundress.

lined picnic basket

YOU WILL NEED
■ 114cm- (45in-) wide Narrow Check (NC 05) –
see below for estimating the quantity
■ 90cm- (35½in-) wide lightweight polyester batting
■ 3m (3¼yds) of 12mm- (½in-) wide elastic   ■ Matching thread
■ Strong thread   ■ Long hand sewing needle
■ Wicker picnic basket   ■ Plastic picnic set

ESTIMATING THE FABRIC QUANTITIES

■ For the main basket lining, measure the inside of the basket from the top of the back edge (near the hinges), down the back, along the base and up the front to the top edge (measurement A). For the width of the main basket lining, measure across the base of the basket from side to side (measurement B). Allow for a rectangle of fabric measuring A by B, plus a 3cm (1¼in) hem allowance on all sides.

■ For the basket side linings, measure the depth of the inside of the basket down the side (measurement C) and across the width from corner to corner (measurement D). Allow for two rectangles of fabric measuring C by D, plus a 3cm (1¼in) hem allowance on all sides.

■ For the basket lid lining, measure the inside of the lid from side to side (measurement E) and back to front (measurement F). Allow for a rectangle of fabric measuring E by F only.

■ For the elasticated straps allow for a strip the width of the fabric by 13cm (5in).

TO MAKE

1 From the checked fabric cut out the lining pieces to the measurements worked out, see left. For the batting cut out a main piece to measurement A by B and two side pieces measurement C by D (do not add on any hem allowances). For the lid, cut one piece measurement E by F and trim away 3cm (1¼in) from all sides.

2 On a flat surface lay out the main lining fabric piece, wrong side up, and place the main batting piece centrally on top. Smooth out layers to remove any wrinkles. Fold over the hem allowances along each side on to the batting and pin in place. Using a large herringbone stitch (see Technique know-how, page 92) catch the fabric hems to the batting around each edge. Remove pins. Make up the two sides and lid panel in the same way.

3 Cut three strips of fabric 4cm- (1½in-) wide, by the width of the fabric. Press one long edge on each strip 6mm (¼in) to the wrong side. Cut elastic into three equal lengths and place one piece centrally on to wrong side of one strip. Fold the long raw edge of the strip over the elastic and then fold the pressed edge over to cover the raw edge and enclose the elastic.

Place this under your machine foot and sew a few stitches to secure down the centre, stopping with your needle down through the fabric.

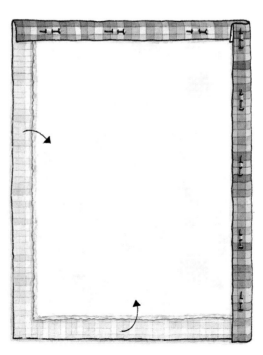

Working on a short section at a time, fold the fabric strip over the elastic and hold with one hand, then gently pull on the elastic to tension it. Stitch along this section and then stop with needle down through work. Continue covering elastic in this manner to base of fabric strip, then repeat to cover remaining pieces of elastic.

4 Lay out the padded lid lining on a flat surface and arrange your plates and cutlery on it, as you would like them to sit. Cut elasticated strips to fit across the plates and around the cutlery, allowing for a 2cm (¾in) hem at each end. Mark positions of elasticated straps on the lid lining with pins. Remove plates and cutlery, then folding over 1cm (⅜in) hem at each end, stitch the elasticated straps in place by stitching around the folded ends in a small square shape.

5 Place the padded main basket lining in the basket and mark the lower edge of the front and back (where it bends for the base)

with a row of pins. Remove lining and work out positions for remaining pieces of your picnic set on the back 'wall' section of the lining. Mark, and stitch straps in place as shown in step 4 for lid.

6 With right sides together, and matching up base corners to pin-lines, whipstitch (see Technique know-how, page 92) the basket side linings to the main lining along the lower edges. Fold the main lining up at both the front and back and whipstitch these to the side edges of the lining sides.

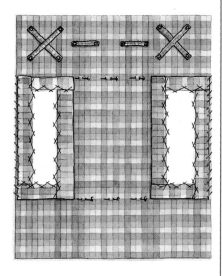

7 Insert lining into basket, and using the strong thread and long needle, hand stitch the top edge of the lining to the wicker basket. Repeat along the lower back edge of the lining. Place the lid lining centrally on the lid and stitch in place around all edges. Catch lid lining to wicker basket at each point where elasticated straps are stitched. Insert picnic set under straps. Now you're ready for a picnic!

summer sarong

YOU WILL NEED
■ **1.8m (2yds) of 114cm- (45in-) wide Broad Check (BC 01)**
■ **Matching thread**

TO MAKE

Trim off the selvedges along each side of the fabric's edge, following one of the check lines. Press a double 1cm (⅜in) hem to wrong side along each edge of the fabric and machine stitch in place.

49

pull on sunhat &
quilted sunglasses case

Sunglasses and a hat are both necessary items for the beach these days.
Make a matching set with our cotton pull-on hat and softly quilted
sunglasses cover. They are both lined with a bright, sunshine yellow lining,
and will roll up, taking little room in your luggage.

pull on sunhat

YOU WILL NEED
- 50cm (⅝yd) of 114cm- (45in-) wide Narrow Check (NC 05)
- 20cm (¼yd) of 114cm- (45in-) wide Sunshine (SC 35) Shot Cotton
- 70cm (¾yd) of 90cm- (35½in-) wide lightweight iron-on interfacing
- Contrasting thread ■ Templates on pages 109, 110 & 111

Note: A 1.5cm (⅝in) seam allowance is included throughout. Stitch seams with right sides together, unless otherwise stated.

TO MAKE

1 Using the templates cut out four sides, one top and two brims, from checked fabric and interfacing. From the Sunshine Shot Cotton cut four sides and one top for the hat lining.

2 Press interfacing to the wrong side of each checked piece of fabric. Stitch the four checked hat sides together matching notches, to form a ring. Press seams open and topstitch turnings in place, working 6mm (¼in) each side of the seam lines. Stitch top edge of the joined hat sides to the checked hat top, right sides together. Clip turnings and press them towards the hat sides. Topstitch turnings in place around the hat sides, close to the seamline.

3 Stitch hat brims together at short, notched centre back edges, to form two circular brims. Press seams open, then stitch brims together around outer circular edges, right sides together, matching centre back seams. Clip into the curved seam turnings and trim them down to 6mm (¼in) in depth. Turn through to right side and press seamed edges flat. Baste inner raw circular edges together and starting at outer edge, work six rows of circular topstitching, spacing each row 6mm (¼in) apart.

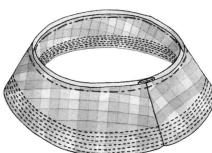

4 Stitch the brim to lower edge of the hat, matching the centre back seam with one hat side seam. Clip curved brim turnings and press up towards the hat sides. Make the hat lining following step 2 see left, omitting references to interfacing and topstitching.

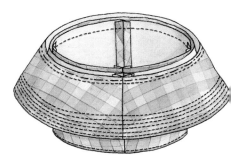

5 Press the lower edge of the hat lining 1.5cm (⅝in) to the wrong side and place lining inside hat, with wrong sides together. Matching hat side seams and lining up the pressed lower edge with brim stitchline, pin and baste the lining in place around its lower edge. Working from the right side of the hat, topstitch the lining in place around the hat sides, stitching close to the brim seamline. Remove basting stitches.

quilted sunglasses case

YOU WILL NEED

■ 35 x 35cm (14 x14in) Narrow Check (NC 05)
■ 30cm (⅓yd) of 114cm- (45in-) wide Sunshine (SC 35) Shot Cotton
■ 30cm (⅓yd) of 90cm- (35 ½in-) wide lightweight polyester batting
■ 30cm (⅓yd) of fine (No 2) piping cord   ■ Contrasting thread
■ Template on page 112

TO MAKE

1 Cut a piece of batting 35 x 35cm (14 x14in). On a flat surface, lay out the batting and then place the checked fabric, right side up, on top. Smooth out the layers to remove any wrinkles. Pin the layers together at the corners and midpoints on each side. Baste layers together close to the edge. Then baste horizontally and vertically across the whole piece to from a cross at the centre.

2 Working on the fabric side, stitch rows of quilting both vertically and horizontally across the piece using the checks on the fabric as a guide. Space each row of stitching two checks apart.

3 Lay quilted fabric face down, and using the template trace out the sunglasses case, placing the grainline along one of the quilted stitch lines. Cut out. From the Sunshine Shot Cotton cut another sunglasses case, for the lining. From the remaining Sunshine Shot Cotton, cut out and make up the length of piping (see the Technique know-how section, on page 89). Baste piping to top edge of quilted sunglasses case, between the two dots.

4 Clip into the curved seam turnings on the top edge of the sunglasses case and press them to the wrong side. With right sides together, fold sunglasses case in half, and stitch the raw side and lower curved edges together, between dots, with a 1cm (⅜in) seam

allowance. Clip curved seam turnings, turn through to right side and lightly press. Fold lining in half, and stitch side seams together between dots.

5 With wrong sides facing, slip the lining inside the quilted sunglasses case, matching up the side seams. Turn under a 1cm (⅜in) hem along the curved top edge of the lining and slipstitch (see the Technique know-how section, on page 91) the folded edge to the piping seam turnings on the inside of the sunglasses case.

CREATIVE TIP

If you're not using checked fabric, then for step 2 draw parallel lines on the batting side, spaced 2cm (¾in) apart. Turn the fabric 90 degrees and draw parallel lines spaced as before in the opposite direction to form a grid for quilting.

summer flowers

Wander through an English garden at midsummer and you'll marvel at the blowsy masses of colour that scramble riotously through the herbaceous border. Magenta coloured phloxes, the pinks of roses and lilies and the hot scarlet of geraniums are brought into harmony by the different greens of their foliage. Bring the colours of a summer garden into your living room with soft furnishings made from sumptuous flower patterns designed by Kaffe Fassett. The perennial favourites of Flower Lattice and Floral Dance are offset by the greens of Artichoke in showy clusters of appliquéd cushions and petal-headed curtains.

appliquéd cushions

These appliquéd cushions use floral motifs cut from printed fabric, which are stitched onto plain or striped backgrounds. This technique, which was popular in the 18th century, is called Broderie Perse, named because of its similarity to Persian embroidery. We've brought the idea up to date with three cushion designs for your home.

bordered appliquéd cushions

YOU WILL NEED
- 45cm (½yd) of 114cm- (45in-) wide Rowan Stripe (RS 07)
- 30cm (⅓yd) of 114cm- (45in-) wide Custard (SC 30) Shot Cotton
- 45cm (½yd) of 114cm- (45in-) wide Apple (SC 39) Shot Cotton
- A piece of Flower Lattice (GP 11- SU) containing a whole large flower motif ■ 46cm (18in) square cushion pad
- Paper-backed fusible web ■ Matching thread

TO MAKE

Border cushion

1 From the Rowan stripe cut a 31cm (12¼in) square. Iron the paper-backed fusible web to the wrong side of the floral fabric and carefully cut around the outer edge of the flower. Peel the backing paper off the motif and place it centrally in the centre of the striped square. Press in place. Set your sewing machine to a medium-sized, close zigzag stitch, and using toning thread, stitch around the edges of the motif, enclosing all raw edges.

2 From the plain yellow fabric cut two short borders 11.5 x 31cm (4½ x 12¼in) and two long borders 11.5 x 48cm (4½ x 19in). With right sides together and taking a 1.5cm (⅝in) seam allowance, stitch one long edge of each short border to two opposite edges of the

appliquéd square. Press the seams open. Then stitch one long edge of each long border to the remaining sides of the square. Press seams open.

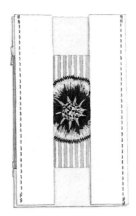

3 From the Apple Shot Cotton cut out two back panels 35 x 48cm (13¾ x 19in). Press a double turned 1.5cm (⅝in) hem to the wrong side down one long edge of each back panel and machine stitch in place.

4 Lay front cover right side uppermost on a flat surface and place the back panels face down on top, raw edges level and hemmed edges overlapping at the centre. Baste the cover pieces together around all sides and machine stitch in place with a 1.5cm (⅝in) seam allowance. Clip corners, remove basting stitches and turn to right side. Push out corners well and press seamed edges flat. Insert cushion pad through back opening.

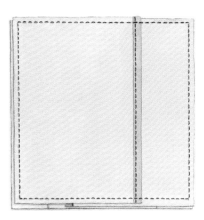

Striped cushion

1 From the plain Custard fabric cut one central strip 18 x 48cm (7 x 19in). Iron the paper-backed fusible web to the wrong side of the floral fabric and carefully cut around the outer edge of three flowers. Peel the backing paper off the motifs and arrange them along the strip of fabric, placing one centrally and the others at each side. Using a hot iron, press in place. Set your sewing machine to a medium-sized, close zigzag stitch, and using toning thread, stitch around the edges of each motif, enclosing all raw edges.

2 From the striped fabric cut two strips of fabric 18 x 48cm (7 x 19in) with the stripes running parallel to the short edges. With right sides together and taking a 1.5cm (⅝in) seam allowance, stitch one long edge of each striped strip to each long side of the plain appliquéd strip. Press the seams open.

striped & squared appliquéd cushions

YOU WILL NEED FOR STRIPED CUSHION
■ 23cm (¼yd) of 114cm- (45in-) wide Rowan
Stripe (RS 07)   ■ 23cm (¼yd) of 114cm- (45in-) wide
Custard (SC 30), 45cm (½yd) of Apple (SC 39) and
30cm (⅓yd) of Rosy (SC 32) Shot Cottons
■ A piece of Flower Lattice (GP 11- SU) with
three large flowers

YOU WILL NEED FOR SQUARE CUSHION
■ 30cm (⅓yd) of 114cm- (45in-) wide Rowan
Stripe (RS 07)   ■ 30cm (⅓yd) of 114cm- (45in-) wide Apple
(SC 39), 45cm (½yd) of Custard (SC 30) and 30cm (⅓yd) of
Raspberry (SC 08) Shot Cottons
■ A piece of Flower Lattice (GP 11- SU) with
four large flower

YOU WILL NEED FOR BOTH CUSHIONS
■ 2m (2¼yds) of medium (No 3) piping cord
■ 46cm (18in) square cushion pad
■ Paper-backed fusible web
■ Matching thread

3 From the pink Shot Cotton cut out and make up the piping cord. Baste the cord to the right side of appliquéd front cover around the outer edge (see Technique know-how section, page 89).

4 Make up the back panels and complete the cushion cover following steps 3 and 4 of the bordered appliqué cushion, but use a piping or zipper foot on your machine when stitching the outer edges of the cushion together.

Square cushion

1 Cut two squares 25.5cm (10in) from both the plain Apple and striped fabric. Iron the paper-backed fusible web to the wrong side of the floral fabric and carefully cut around the outer edge of four flowers. Peel the backing paper off the motifs and arrange one in the centre of each square. Using a hot iron press in place. Set your sewing machine to a medium-sized, close zigzag stitch, and using toning thread, stitch around the edges of each motif, enclosing all raw edges.

2 With right sides facing and taking a 1.5cm (⅝in) seam allowance, stitch a plain and a striped appliqué square together along one edge. Press seam open. Repeat with remaining appliquéd squares.

3 To form the cushion front, place the joined squares on top of each other with right sides facing, making sure the plain squares lie on top of the striped ones. With central seams matching stitch the squares together along one long edge. Press seam open.

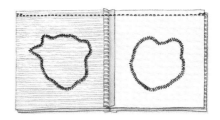

4 From the Raspberry Shot Cotton cut out and make up the piping cord. Baste the cord to the right side of appliquéd front cover around the outer edge (see Technique know-how section, page 89).

5 Make up the back panels from the Custard Shot Cotton and complete the cushion cover following steps 3 and 4 of the bordered appliqué cushion, but use a piping or zipper foot on your machine when stitching the outer edges of the cushion together.

padded window seat
& button bolster

Turn a deep window seat into a comfortable place to sit and relax with
a squashy foam filled box cushion, defined round its edges with contrast
colour piping. A matching bolster cushion sets it off perfectly with its
gathered ends, finished off with large covered buttons.

padded window seat

YOU WILL NEED

■ 114cm- (45in-) wide Artichokes (GP 07-L) –
see below for estimating the quantity
■ 7.5cm (3in) thick high-density flame-retardant foam pad –
see below for estimating the quantity
■ 90cm (1yd) of 114cm- (45cm-) wide Lilac (SC 36) Shot Cotton
■ Medium (No 3) piping cord, enough to go around top and bottom
edges of foam pad ■ Matching thread
■ Large sheet of brown paper or newsprint

ESTIMATING THE QUANTITIES

■ It is best to make a template for your foam pad which you can take along to your foam supplier and they will cut it to size. Lay the sheet of paper over your seating area and trace around the shape. Cut out the template and replace it back on the seat to check the shape.

■ Use the template also to work out your fabric quantity. You will need a top and a bottom of the same size as the template, plus a 1.5cm (⅝in) seam allowance all around.

■ The side gusset is 10.5cm (4¼in) deep (the depth of the foam, plus seam allowance). To find the length of the gusset, measure around the outer edges of the template. You will need to join fabric widths to obtain the correct length.

TO MAKE

1 From the print fabric cut out one top and bottom piece and the side gusset pieces. Join the gusset pieces to obtain the correct length: try to position seams so that they will match up to any front corners.

2 From the Lilac Shot Cotton cut out and make up a length of piping cord to fit the outer edges of both the top and bottom cover pieces. Baste a length to the right side of each piece (see Technique know-how section, page 89).

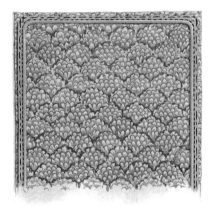

3 Once the cord is basted in place, seam the short ends of the gusset together to form a ring. Place the gusset around the foam pad to check that it fits. With right sides together, pin and baste the gusset around the piped top section, snipping into the gusset seam allowance at each corner to allow it to bend. Stitch pieces together close to the cord using a piping or zipper foot on your machine.

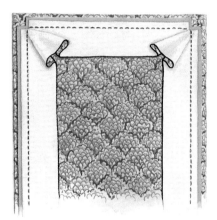

4 With right sides together, pin and baste the other side of the gusset around the piped bottom section, leaving a large opening along the back edge and snipping into the gusset seam allowance at each corner. Machine stitch in place as before.

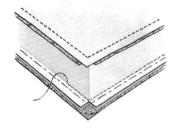

5 Turn the cover right side out. Insert pad through back opening pushing it well into the corners and making sure that the seam allowances are not twisted and that they all lay flat against the gusset. Slipstitch the opening edges closed to enclose the pad (see Technique know-how section, page 91).

button bolster

ESTIMATING THE FABRIC QUANTITY

■ Measure the length, circumference and diameter of the bolster pad.

■ On the sheet of paper draw out the main pattern piece, the length by the circumference, and add a 1.5cm (⅝in) seam allowance to all sides. Cut out pattern piece.

■ For the end pieces draw out a rectangle the length of the circumference by half the diameter. Add a 2cm (¾in) seam allowance to one long side and a 1.5cm (⅝in) seam allowance to the remaining sides. Cut out pattern piece.

TO MAKE

1 From the print fabric cut out one main piece and two end pieces. With right sides together, fold the main fabric piece in half across its width, bringing the shorter edges together. Stitch the shorter edges together with a 1.5cm (⅝cm) seam allowance, to form a cylinder. Press seam turnings open and turn to right side.

2 Neaten one long edge of an end piece and with right sides together, fold it in half, bringing the short edges together. Stitch the short edges together to form a cylinder, starting 3.5cm (1⅜in) down from the neatened edge to allow for an opening channel. Press

seamed edges open and opening edges 1.5cm (⅝in) to wrong side. Repeat with remaining end piece.

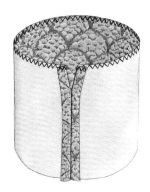

3 From the Lilac Shot Cotton cut out and make up the piping cord. Cut the cord into two equal lengths and baste a length to the right side of each circular end of the main piece (see Technique know-how section, page 89).

4 Once the cord is basted in place, slip an end piece over the top, with right sides together, seams matching and raw edges level. Pin, baste and then stitch the two pieces together close to the cord, using the piping or zipper foot on your

machine. Repeat at opposite end with the remaining end piece.

5 Press a 2cm (¾in) hem to the wrong side around each neatened end of the cover and machine stitch in place to form a channel. Slip the bolster pad inside the cover, lining up the ends of the bolster with the piped seams.

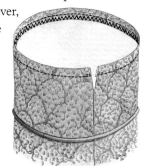

6 Cut the cotton tape into two equal lengths. Using the bodkin or tapestry needle, thread a length of tape through each channel, pulling the tape tightly to gather the ends at the centre. Knot tape ends together and cut off excess tape. Cover the self-cover buttons with print fabric following the manufacturer's instructions. Hand-stitch a button to the centre of each gathered end.

petal curtains & upholstered stool

These deep, scalloped curtains are interlined with a warm layer.
Although there's more effort involved in making interlined curtains, the
finished result is well worth it. The scalloped tops fold over to form a
pretty valance, which is attached to the pole with rings. Use a
flowery remnant of fabric to cover a footstool and finish off the
edges with floral braid.

petal curtains

YOU WILL NEED
■ 114cm- (45in-) wide Floral Dance (GP 12-PK) – see below for estimating the quantity ■ 114cm- (45in-) wide Custard (SC 30) Shot Cotton – see below for estimating the quantity
■ 114cm- (45in-) wide curtain interlining – see below for estimating the quantity ■ 2.5cm- (1in-) wide bias binding in Rosy (SC 32) Shot Cotton, two and half times the finished width of the curtain – see 'Making bias binding' in the Technique know-how, on page 89 ■ Matching thread
■ Large curtain rings ■ Template from page 113
■ Brown paper or newsprint

ESTIMATING THE FABRIC QUANTITY

Measure your window to find the finished width and length of the curtains (see 'Measuring up for curtains' in the Technique know-how, page 86). Add 60cm (24in) to the length measurement for the overhang at the top, and 8cm (3in) for a base hem. For wide windows like ours you will need to allow two widths of fabric for each curtain. For narrower ones you should be fine with just one width.

TO MAKE

1 From the print fabric, plain fabric and interlining cut out the required number of widths, to the length measurement you have just calculated. Join the fabric widths if necessary to obtain correct curtain width, with plain straight seams, and the interlining widths with lapped seams (see the Technique know-how section, on page 89).

2 Lay the main print fabric out wrong side up on a large flat surface with the base edge nearest you. Press over a single 8cm (3in) hem along the base edge and a single 6cm (2⅜in) hem down the side edges. Open hems out; do not stitch.

3 Lay the interlining on top of the fabric with side and base edges level. Working from the leading side edge (the one that will be at the centre of the window when the curtains are drawn), fold the interlining back on itself along the pressline. Using herringbone stitches (see the Technique know-how section, on page 92), secure the interlining to the fabric along the foldline of the leading edge, taking one thread at a time so stitches don't show on the right side.

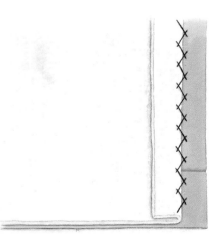

4 Lock the interlining to the main fabric at the centre of each fabric width, and also at centre seam allowances if you have them. To do this, fold the interlining back in a straight line along the first half width and work locking stitches up the curtain's length from the bottom (see the Technique know-how section, on page 92) stopping 15cm (6in) from the top. Continue to lock interlining to fabric across to opposite edge of the curtain, pinning each section as you work, to stop the layers separating. When you reach the opposite side, trim away any excess interlining and herringbone in place in the same manner as the leading edge. Herringbone the base edge of interlining to the base hem foldline in the same way.

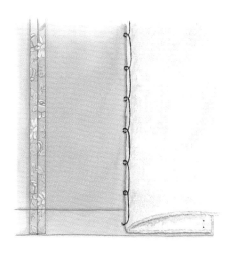

5 Fold over the base and side hems and pin in place. Mitre the base corners (see the Technique know-how section, on page 90). Slipstitch mitred edges together and herringbone stitch the base and side hems in place (see the Technique know-how section, on page 92).

6 Lay the plain lining fabric out, wrong side up, on a large flat surface with base nearest you. Press over a single 8cm (3in) hem along the base edge. Press a single 2cm (¾in) hem down each side edge, then press these over a further 4cm (1½in) to the wrong side.

7 Open out the second fold of each lining side hem. With wrong sides facing, lay the main curtain on top of the lining, with folded base edges level and side edges level with the lining side presslines. Working from leading edge, fold the lining side hem over onto the right side of the main curtain to form a contrasting border down the side edge. Pin, baste and

slipstitch (see the Technique know-how section, on page 91) the lining hem in place.

8 Lock the main curtain to the lining across the width as shown in step 4 for the interlining, finishing off the opposite side hem in the same way as the leading edge, to form another contrasting border.

9 Starting 5cm (2in) from one side edge, baste the lining hem edge 1cm (⅜in) to the wrong side. Keeping the raw edges level, slipstitch (see the Technique know-how section, on page 91) the basted lining edge to the main curtain hem. Remove basting stitches.

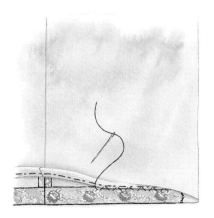

10 Using the brown paper or newsprint complete the template shape as shown on page 113. Then using the whole template as a guide, make sure that the finished width of the curtain is divisible by the width of the template. If not, adjust template slightly. Lay the curtain out flat, wrong side up, with the top raw edges nearest you. Starting at one side edge, mark around the

template to form petal shapes, as shown in diagram. Remove template and cut along the marked line. Working close to the edge, baste the top raw edges together.

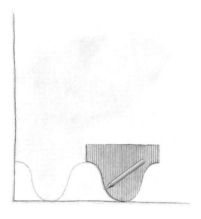

11 To bind the raw edges of the shaped top edge, place the binding right side down on the lining side of the curtain. Open out one folded edge of the binding, and with raw edges level, pin and baste the binding place around the shaped edge, leaving 1cm (⅜in) of binding extending at each side edge. Machine stitch binding in place along the binding foldline.

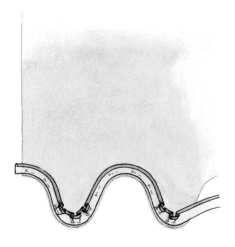

12 Fold the binding to the front of the curtain (this side will not be visible when the curtain is hung) and pin the folded edge of the binding all around the shaped edge. Neatly slipstitch the binding in place all along the top edge of the curtain (see the Technique know-how section, on page 91). Tuck in raw ends at the side edges and slipstitch in place. Press the binding flat.

13 Measure approximately 50cm (20in) down the curtain from the shaped end and fold the curtain over to the main print side at this point. The shaped edge will fall on the front of the curtain and form a valance. Press along the line. Double check that the curtain is not too long or short for the window – adjust depth of valance fold if necessary. Space the curtain rings out equally along the width of the curtain and stitch them in place along the top folded edge. Hang the curtain, by threading the rings on to a curtain pole.

upholstered stool

ESTIMATING THE QUANTITIES

■ It is best to make a template for your foam pad which you can take along to your foam supplier and they will cut it to size. Lay the sheet of paper over your stool and trace around the shape. Cut out the template and replace on the stool to check the shape.

■ Use the template also to work out your fabric quantity. You will need enough to cover the top of your foam pad plus the depth of your foam all around and a little extra to allow for fitting.

TO MAKE

Using the spray glue attach the foam to the top of the stool. Place the fabric centrally over the top. Secure fabric in place with staples or tacks, fastening them in on alternate sides to keep the tension even. Fold the fabric neatly at the corners and fasten in place. Trim away raw edges of fabric to fit, and cover the staples or tacks with the decorative braid, glued in place.

CREATIVE TIP

Make a generous allowance when cutting out fabric, allow for at least 5cm (2in) on all sides. This will make it much easier to get the right tension on the fabric.

Make sure you get the tension smooth and regular over the whole seat. If the fabric is not taught enough it will sag with use, too tight and fabric can split away from the tacks or staples.

Staples are a quick way of fastening fabric in place, but beginners may find it easier to use tacks. By hammering tacks in halfway only at first, means you can remove them more easily if they need to be repositioned .

Fold corners and tack into position for a neat, professional finish, then slipstitch the corners together, making sure that fold openings are not visible from the front.

Make sure you hammer all the tacks 'home' to anchor the fabric firmly in place. Always hammer the heads flat, not at an angle, to prevent them cutting through fabric.

neapolitan pastels

Crumbly Battenberg cake with almond flavoured marzipan, creamy ices that melt in the mouth, both share the same soft colours. Water-based paints to tint a stack of flowerpots in chalky colours or reels of sewing cottons in iridescent shades – take a look around you at everyday things that can inspire home-based sewing projects. For a homely and welcoming kitchen use shot cottons in myriad pastel shades to make everything from a harlequin quilted tea cosy to the simplest of fabric heart shapes filled with herbs. Try your hand at a machine embroidered tray cloth or stitch a set of jam pot covers.

embroidered tray cloth
& three colour curtain

Lay a tray with this pretty, machine-embroidered tray cloth. The simple shapes are carefully snipped away after stitching to show the contrast colour backing. If you're still a beginner why not start with our easy three-tone curtain. Three panels are stitched together and the raw edges bound with a contrasting shade — it couldn't be easier, and looks brilliant!

embroidered tray cloth

YOU WILL NEED

■ 50cm x 57cm (20in x 22½in) of Blush (SC 28) Shot Cotton
■ 50cm x 57cm (20in x 22½in) of Apple (SC 39) Shot Cotton
■ 1.5m (1⅔yd) of 2cm- (¾in-) wide bias binding in Rosy (SC 32)
Shot Cotton – see 'Making bias binding' in the Technique know-how,
on page 89 ■ Matching thread ■ Contrasting thread
■ Dressmakers' carbon paper ■ Embroidery motif on page 109
■ Embroidery hoop ■ Small pair of sharp scissors
■ Tear-away embroidery backing

TO MAKE

1 Using dressmakers' carbon paper, trace the embroidery motif on to one side of the Blush fabric piece, placing it about 10cm (4in) in from one corner. Place a piece of tear-away embroidery backing behind the design and clip both layers into an embroidery hoop, fabric side up. Place design in hoop under your machine foot and stitch around design lines using a very close zigzag stitch and contrasting thread.

2 Remove embroidery from hoop and tear away the backing. Using a small pair of sharp scissors, and taking care not to cut the stitches, trim away the fabric inside the embroidered loops.

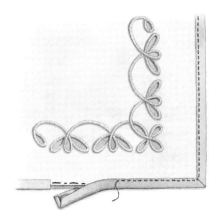

3 From the Apple green fabric cut out a rectangle 28 x 42cm (11 x 16½in); trim the embroidered Blush fabric piece to the same size. Place the two pieces wrong sides facing and baste together around the outer edges.

4 Finish the edges of the tray cloth with bias binding, folded in half lengthways with turnings inside and machine stitched over the raw edges. Fold binding carefully at each corner to make a 90-degree turn and finish the ends off neatly by pressing them 1cm (⅜in) to the wrong side and butting them up close together.

CREATIVE TIP

If you own a computerised sewing machine that does automatic embroidery designs, then you'll probably have some motifs of your own that you can use to decorate your tray cloth – so try experimenting with one of these too.

Our tray cloth embroidery design is taken from: Husqvarna Viking, Designer 1 Sampler Diskette 1.10

three colour curtains

YOU WILL NEED
■ **Three Shot Cotton fabrics, 114cm- (45in-) wide
(see below for estimating the quantity). We used Apple (SC 39),
Rosy (SC 32) and Lilac (SC 36)
■ Matching threads**

ESTIMATING THE FABRIC QUANTITY

■ Measure your cupboard opening to find the finished width and length of the curtain. Multiply your width by 1½ to allow for some fabric fullness. Then divide this measurement into three to find the finished width of each panel. To the panel width, add a 1.5cm (⅝in) seam allowance to each side.

■ To the length measurement add 9cm (3½in) for top and base hem allowances.

■ Finally allow for two contrasting side strips, the cut length of your curtain by 7cm (2¾in) wide.

TO MAKE

1 Cut out the curtain panels and join them together with French seams (see the Technique know-how section, on page 88). Press seams to one side.

2 Press a 1.5cm (⅝in) hem to the wrong side down both long edges of the side strips. Open out one of the pressed hems on one strip, and with right sides together and raw edges matching, lay it along one side edge of the curtain. Pin, baste and machine stitch strip in place along the pressline.

3 Fold strip over the edge on to the wrong side of the curtain, lining the pressed edge up with machine stitchline. Pin and then slipstitch this edge to the curtain along machine stitches. Repeat steps 2 and 3 to neaten the opposite side edge of the curtain. Press strips flat.

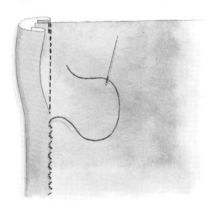

4 Press a 1cm (⅜in) hem to wrong side along the top and base edges of the curtain. Then press over a further 3cm (1¼in) hem to the wrong side along the top edge and a further 4cm (1½in) along the base. Machine stitch in place. Slipstitch the open side edges of the base hem together, but leave the top side edges open to form a slot heading.

HANGING THE CURTAIN

For a cheap option thread the curtain onto a simple net wire with hooks screwed to the top, or sides of the opening.

For an instant solution use an expanding net rod, which is spring-loaded allowing it to wedge itself between the two walls.

If your curtain needs to be drawn back often, then screw a lightweight plastic curtain track to the underside of the work surface, and stitch a narrow gathered heading tape to the top of the curtain. Hang using curtain hooks.

harlequin tea cosy
& herby hearts

For those who have never tackled patchwork, this pretty tea cosy is ideal as a first project as it's simply made from basic squares of colour and hand-stitched with contrasting thread afterwards. Even easier to sew is a set of heart shapes that are filled with dried herbs. Hang them in a warm place to bring a gorgeous scent to your kitchen all year round.

harlequin tea cosy

YOU WILL NEED

■ 15cm (⅛yd) of 114cm- (45in-) wide Apple (SC 39), Rosy (SC 32),
Lilac (SC 36) and Custard (SC 30) Shot Cottons
■ 30cm (⅓yd) of 114cm- (45in-) wide Duck Egg (SC 26) Shot Cotton
■ 76cm (30in) of 2cm- (¾in-) wide bias binding in Duck Egg (SC 26) Shot
Cotton, see 'Making bias binding' in the Technique know-how, on page 89
■ Matching thread ■ Templates on page 108
■ 30cm (⅓yd) of 90cm- (35½in-) wide lightweight batting ■ Pink, apple
green and custard yellow stranded embroidery threads

TO MAKE

1 Using the template cut out 12 patchwork squares in Rosy and 11 each in Lilac, Custard and Apple. Using a 6mm (¼in) seam allowance, stitch the squares together in nine rows of five squares, alternating the colours. Stitch three rows starting and finishing with a Rosy square, two rows starting and finishing with an Apple square, two with Lilac squares and two with Custard squares. Press all seams open.

2 Using a 6mm (¼in) seam allowance, join the nine strips together to form the patchwork top, matching seams and alternating the colours along the top and bottom edges, i.e. pink, green, lilac, yellow, pink, green lilac, yellow and pink. Press the patchwork top.

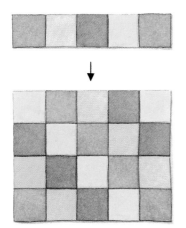

3 On a flat surface lay out the patchwork top face down and place the batting on top. Smooth out the layers to remove any wrinkles, then pin the layers together at the corners and midpoints of each side. Baste layers together close to the edge, then work horizontal and vertical rows of basting stitches over the entire patchwork, spaced approximately 10cm (4in) apart.

3 Working from the right side, machine quilt along all the seams of the patchwork. This is called stitching-in-the-ditch. Once you have quilted the entire piece, remove the basting stitches.

4 Using a photocopier scale up the tea cosy template on page 108, as indicated on the page. Using the full-sized template and making sure you place the patchwork grainline following the right direction, cut out two cosy pieces from the quilted patchwork fabric. Using the same template, but following the lining grainline, cut out two lining pieces from the Duck Egg fabric.

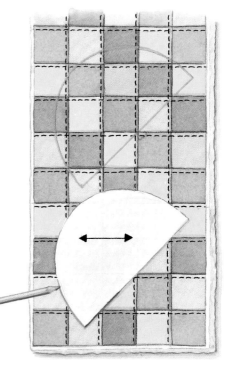

5 Baste layers together close to the edges around the two quilted patchwork pieces of the cosy. Using the stranded embroidery thread, work rows of hand quilting stitches up the centre of each row of patchwork squares in both directions, alternating the colours of the thread.

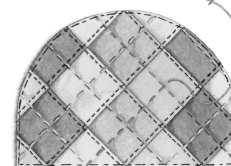

6 Cut a 7.5cm (3in) length from the bias binding and press it in half lengthways with turnings inside. Stitch pressed edges together. Fold strip in half to make a loop and stitch raw ends to right side of one tea cosy piece, placing it at the centre of the curved edge at the notch position marked on the template.

7 Place the two quilted patchwork sections right sides together, then lay the two lining pieces on top. Taking a 1cm (⅜in) seam allowance, pin, baste and machine stitch the layers together around the curved edges only, sandwiching the top loop in place at the same time.

8 Clip into the curved seam turnings and turn cosy through to the right side. Baste the linings to the patchwork at the straight lower edges of the cosy. Finish off the lower edges with the remaining bias binding, folded in half lengthways with turnings inside and machine stitched over the raw edges. For a neat finish to the bias binding, press ends 1cm (⅜in) to the wrong side and butt up close together. Remove any basting stitches that still show.

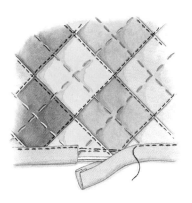

herby hearts

YOU WILL NEED
■ Small pieces of Apple (SC 39), Rosy (SC 32) and Duck egg (SC 26) Shot Cottons ■ Matching thread ■ Template on page 107 ■ Shell buttons ■ Toy stuffing or dried herbs ■ Jute string ■ Fresh or dried herb sprigs

TO MAKE

1 Cut out two heart shapes from one piece of fabric. Place heart shapes right sides together and stitch around the edges with a 6mm (¼in) seam allowance, leaving an opening along one of the straighter sides. Clip into curved seam turnings and turn through to right side.

2 Stuff heart with toy stuffing, or fill with dried herbs, then slipstitch the gap closed (see Technique know-how section, on page 91). Handstitch a shell button to the front of the heart and a sisal hanging loop to the top.

3 Split a length of jute string into its separate strands and use one strand to tie the sprig of fresh or dried herbs on to the hanging loop. Repeat steps 1 to 3 to make hearts from the other coloured fabrics.

ADDING FRAGRANCE

Stuff hearts with dried mixed herbs, rosemary and thyme, or choose lavender or camomile for their therapeutic and calming effects.

Tie on dried citrus peel or stuff with cloves to ward off flies.

Thread dried bay leaves on to the hanging string, or try tying on little bundles of cinnamon sticks.

piped coasters & jam pot covers

A row of tiny running stitches worked by hand neatly finishes off a set of multi-coloured drinks coasters, each one piped in the palest pink. Turn pots of jam into something a bit more special with our appliqué jam pot covers too. Topped with a pearly button and tied with string, they make a perfect gift for friends and family.

piped coasters

YOU WILL NEED

■ Small amounts of Apple (SC 39), Rosy (SC 32), Duck Egg (SC 26), Lilac (SC 36) and Custard (SC 30) Shot Cottons
■ 30cm (⅓yd) of 114cm- (45in-) wide Blush (SC 28) Shot Cotton
■ 3m (3⅓yds) of fine (No 2) piping cord   ■ Matching thread
■ Template on page 107   ■ 30cm (⅓yd) of 90cm- (35½in-) wide medium weight iron-on interfacing   ■ Cream stranded embroidery thread

TO MAKE

1 Using the template cut out two coaster shapes from each colour of Shot Cotton and twelve shapes from the interfacing. Then with a hot iron, press an interfacing piece to the back of each fabric piece.

2 From the remaining Blush Shot Cotton cut out and make up 50cm (19½in) of piping for each coaster and baste a length to the right side of one coaster piece (see Technique know-how section, page 89).

4 Clip into curved seam turnings and turn coaster right side out. Slipstitch the opening edges together and press coaster flat. Thread a needle with a length of the stranded embroidery thread and work a row of small evenly spaced running stitches (see Technique know-how section, on page 92) 6mm (¼in) in from the piped edges. Complete the remaining coasters in the same way.

CREATIVE TIP

Fancy some matching placemats? Then simply scale up your coaster template by 200% on a photocopier and make them up in the same way.

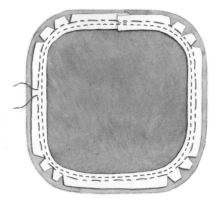

3 Once the cord is basted in place, lay the second piece of the coaster over the first with right sides facing. Pin, baste and machine stitch the two pieces together close to the cord using a piping or zipper foot, and leaving a gap along one side for turning through.

jam pot covers

YOU WILL NEED

■ Small amounts of Apple (SC 39), Rosy (SC 32), Duck Egg (SC 26)
and Lilac (SC 36) Shot Cottons
■ Matching and contrasting threads
■ Templates on page 106
■ Small amount of paper-backed fusible web
■ Shell buttons ■ Jute string ■ Small pair of sharp scissors

1 Using the circular template draw out the jam pot covers on to the various colours of Shot Cotton and cut out, leaving about 1cm (⅜in) outside the line. Set to one side. Using a hot iron, stick some paper-backed fusible web to each of the remaining pieces of Shot Cotton. Using the template and a soft pencil, trace off the heart shapes on to the paper backing side of each fabric and cut them out.

2 Remove the paper backing from each heart and place one in the centre of each circle. Press hearts in place using a hot iron.

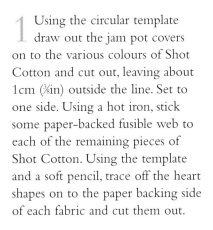

3 Set your sewing machine to a medium-sized, close zigzag stitch and, using matching or contrasting thread, stitch around the edges of each heart, enclosing the raw edges.

4 Using a contrasting thread, zigzag stitch around the drawn line of the circle, then carefully trim away the edges of the fabric up to the stitches, using the small scissors.

5 Stitch a button to the centre of each heart and tie covers to jam pots using a length of the jute string.

technique know-how

Like learning any skill, the secret of successful sewing for the home is to acquire a set of techniques that will stand you in good stead. In this chapter you will find everything you need to make all the projects in this book, from sewing a simple seam to making professional-looking bias binding and piping, how to measure up for curtains or execute hand embroidery techniques. Whether you're new to the craft or just wanting to expand your sewing skills, our illustrations will guide you through the steps. If you're puzzled by some of the terms we've used, just look them up in the glossary and all will become clear.

measuring up for curtains

It is best to have all your tracks and fittings in place before you begin to measure, including carpets for full-length curtains.

For accuracy use a long, retractable steel tape measure and ask someone to help you when measuring larger windows.

Take your time when measuring up. It's important to get the measuring correct to avoid expensive mistakes when buying and cutting out your fabric. Take your finished length measurement a few times across the window, as the floors can run out of square, and check whether your window is true by measuring the width at both the top and the bottom. Check every measurement twice, but don't worry unduly, as small measuring mistakes can usually be rectified.

GENERAL MEASURING UP

The two basic measurements you need to find out before estimating how much fabric you're going to need are:

■ The length of the curtain from the track or pole to the floor (measurement B) or windowsill (measurement C), depending on what you have in mind.

■ The length of the curtain track or pole (measurement A), plus any overlap arms at the centre if your track has them.

CURTAIN LENGTH

■ For curtains hung from an exposed track, you'll need to work out where your heading tape will finish in relation to your track. If you're not sure, hook a piece of the heading tape on to your track and measure down from the top of your tape.

■ For curtains hung from a pole, measure the length from the base of the curtain ring.

■ For full-length curtains, deduct 1cm (⅜in) from measurement B (see diagram A) for clearance. If you want to make your curtains drape on the floor, add 5-20cm (2-8in) to measurement B.

■ For sill-length curtains, try to make them hang just below the sill, as this looks more attractive. To do this, add 5-10cm (2-4in) to measurement C. But if your windowsill protrudes out a long way, deduct 1cm (⅜in) from measurement C this will allow the curtains to hang clear.

CURTAIN FULLNESS AND HEADING TAPES

Before you can work out your fabric quantity, you will need to decide whether your curtain is to be gathered at the top or if it's to have hardly any fullness, as in tab top curtains and eyelet styles.

Gathered styles usually require a heading tape. These contain pockets for inserting hooks and have draw cords running through them. After the tape is attached to the curtain, the cords are pulled up to gather the fabric to your finished curtain width.

■ Standard heading is 2.5cm (1in) deep and needs to be 1½ to 2 times the length of your track or pole. It has one row of pockets and is usually applied 3cm (1¼in) from the top edge of the curtain.

■ Pencil pleat heading is 7.5cm (3in) deep and needs a fabric fullness of 2½ - 3 times the length of your track or pole. It has two or three rows of pockets and is applied close to the top edge of your curtain.

Flatter styles don't usually use heading tapes, but require a fabric fullness of 1¼ - 1½ times the length of your track or pole. These headings are usually hung from poles rather than tracks, by a variety of methods, such as fabric loops (tab tops), eyelets or curtain rings.

HOW MUCH FABRIC DO I NEED?

First, calculate how many fabric widths are needed: for perfectly flat curtains, add your hem allowances to the width measurement and divide this number by the width of your fabric. For curtains with fullness, multiply the length of the track or pole by the fullness required (see Curtain fullness, opposite) and divide this number by the width of your fabric. Round up to the nearest full fabric width.

Next, calculate the total quantity required; add the top and base hem allowances to the length measurement (see individual projects) and multiply this number by the amount of fabric widths you've calculated.

If your fabric has a pattern repeat, add one full design repeat per fabric width after the first width.

stitching basics

PLAIN STRAIGHT SEAMS

This is the most commonly used seam, for joining fabric widths together in curtain making. It is best to take a 2cm (¾in) seam allowance unless otherwise stated.

1 With right sides together, machine stitch along the seamline, reverse stitching for a few stitches at both ends of the seam to secure the threads.

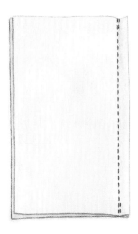

2 For speed and to avoid tacking seams prior to machine stitching, pin seams at right angles to the seamline and then machine slowly over the pins, taking care not to hit one, as it could break the needle.

3 Using a steam iron, press the seam open flat.

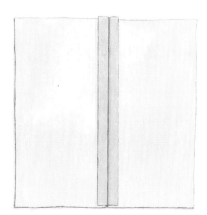

FRENCH SEAMS

This is a self-neatening seam, used mainly on sheer and lightweight fabrics.

1 With wrong sides facing, pin the two edges together and tack if the fabric is slippery. Machine stitch together 6mm (¼in) in from the raw edges.

2 Press the seam open and then refold with right sides together and stitchline placed exactly on the folded edge. Press again and pin, then stitch 1cm (⅜in) in from the seamed edge, enclosing the raw edges. Press finished seam to one side.

FLAT FELL SEAMS

This is another self-neatening seam, which is stronger and flatter than a French seam.

1 With right sides together, stitch a plain straight seam. Press both the seam allowances to one side and then trim the lower seam allowance to 6mm (¼in).

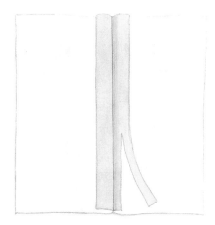

2 Fold the edge of the top seam allowance over the trimmed edge, enclosing it. Press this fold flat. Pin at right angles to the seam and stitch it to the main fabric close to the pressed edge.

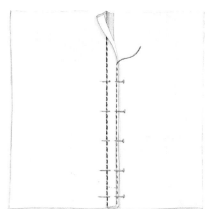

LAPPED SEAMS

Interlinings and bulky fabrics are best joined with lapped seams to give a completely flat finish.

1 With both pieces of fabric right side up, overlap one of the raw edges directly over the other by approximately 2cm (¾in).

2 Machine stitch the two layers together with a straight or zigzag stitch. Trim the raw edges.

MAKING BIAS BINDING

Bias binding is a strip of fabric that is cut on the cross, which means it's cut at an angle to the warp and weft threads of the fabric.

1 To find the bias of the fabric, fold the raw edge (running across the width of the fabric from selvedge to selvedge) down to form a triangle so that it lies parallel to

one of the selvedges. Press and cut along the line.

2 Draw pencil lines parallel to the bias, to the required width. This should be twice the finished flat width of the binding required. Cut along these lines, until you have the required number of strips to form the length to go around the edge of your project.

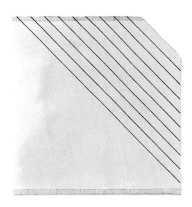

3 To join the strips together, the two ends that are to be joined must be cut at a 45 degree angle, as shown in diagram A. Stitch the pieces together with right sides facing, trim the seam turnings and press the seams open – see diagram B.

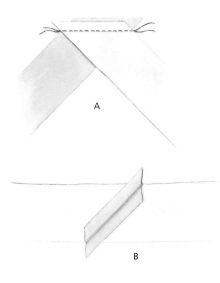

A

B

4 With wrong sides facing, press the strip in half along its length.

5 Open the strip out flat and press the long raw edges over to the wrong side to meet at the central pressline.

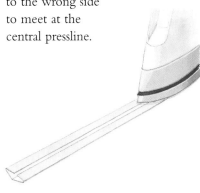

MAKING PIPING

Piping is a fabric-covered cord that adds an attractive finish to seams on cushions, tiebacks and other soft furnishings.

1 To gauge the width of your fabric strip, measure round the cord and allow an extra 3cm (1¼in) for seam allowances. Alternatively, fold a corner of your fabric over the cord and pin, encasing the cord snugly; then measure 1.5cm (⅝in) out from the pin and cut. Then open out the fabric strip to find the correct width.

2 To cut out and make up the fabric strips follow steps 1, 2 and 3 of 'Making bias binding'.

To cover the cord, place the piping cord down the centre of the bias strip on the wrong side. Bring the long edges of the bias strip together around the cord and stitch down the length close to the cord, using a piping or zipper foot on your machine.

3 Baste the piping to the right side of one piece of fabric with the raw edges level and cord facing inwards. If piping is to go around a corner, snip into the piping seam turnings to help it bend. If piping around a curved edge, clip into the piping seam turnings at intervals to allow it to curve smoothly.

4 To pipe a circular seam, the cord ends need to be joined: unpick the machine stitches for about 5cm (2in) at each end and fold back the bias strip. Trim the two cord ends so they butt

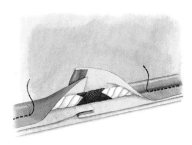

together, then bind the ends together with thread. Turn under 6mm (¼in) of fabric at one end of the bias strip to neaten, and slip this end over the raw opposite end. Baste ends neatly in place.

5 Once the cord is basted in place, lay the second fabric piece over the first with right sides facing and raw edges level. Pin, baste and stitch the two pieces together close to the cord, using the piping or zipper foot on your machine.

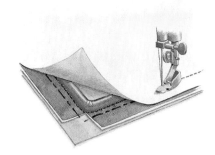

MITRED CORNERS

Mitres form neat flat corners, which are particularly useful for bulky fabrics.

1 Press over the required hem allowances along each side. Open out the hems, then using the inner finished corner point as a pivot and matching up the press lines, fold over a triangular corner.

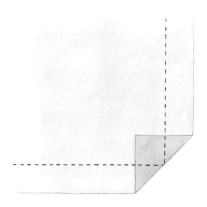

2 Trim away the excess fabric from the folded over corner, to leave a 1.5cm (⅝in) seam allowance.

3 Refold the hems to form the mitre and slipstitch the pressed diagonal edges together.

ELASTICISED SHIRRING

This is a stretchy form of shirring that hugs the body neatly, yet expands and contrasts comfortably with body movements.

1 To work the shirring use an elasticated shirring thread on your machine's bobbin and a regular thread in the needle. Wind the elastic thread on the bobbin by hand, stretching it slightly, until the bobbin is almost full.

2 Set the machine to a 3mm (⅛in) stitch length, and test the results on a scrap of your fabric. Adjust stitch length and tension if necessary. Sometimes to get the desired fullness, the bobbin (elastic) thread must be pulled after stitching, as in gathering.

3 Mark the rows of shirring on the right side of the fabric. As you sew, hold the fabric taut and flat by stretching the fabric in the previous row flat. To secure ends, pull the needle through to the wrong side and tie ends together. Run the machine across the knotted ends to secure.

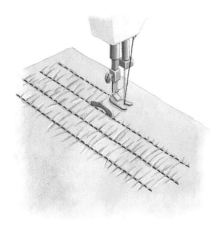

HAND QUILTING

This is best done with the quilt mounted on a quilting frame or hoop, but as long as you have basted the quilt well a frame is not necessary. With the quilt top facing upwards, begin at the centre of the quilt and make even running stitches following the design. It is important to make even stitches on both sides of the quilt than to make small ones. Start and finish your stitching with back stitches and bury the ends of your threads in the batting.

MACHINE QUILTING

Before you start to quilt make sure you have basted your quilt layers together over the entire surface of the quilt and marked out your design.

- Choose a specially designed machine quilting thread which is coated or pre-waxed and allows the thread to glide more easily through the fabric layers.

- Use a size 80 needle and sew a few stitches on a sample to test the stitch length. Fabrics can tear away if the stitches are too small, but large stitches do not have the stretch to tolerate stress on the quilt during use. When the stitch length is right, check the tension. Because the quilt sandwich is thicker than normal, you may need to reduce the tension a little, but make sure the two threads still lock together in the middle.

- For a flat looking quilt, always use a walking or quilting foot on your machine for straight lines. This has a dual feed control, which allows the fabric layers to be fed evenly from the top and bottom, reducing the risk of slippage and puckering.

- It's best to start your quilting at the centre of the quilt and work out towards the borders. Make it easier for yourself by handling the quilt properly. Roll up the excess quilt neatly to fit under your sewing machine arm, and use a table or chair to support the weight of the quilt that hangs down the other side.

Useful hand stitches

Note: The following stitches are worked for a right handed person; simply reverse them if you are left-handed.

BASTING STITCH

This is a temporary stitch used to hold two pieces of fabric together. Make long stitches just inside the stitchline, until you're ready to stitch permanently. Use a bright coloured thread so that it's easy to see when removing.

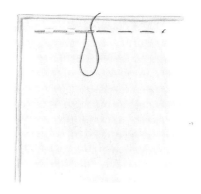

SLIPSTITCH

This stitch is used to join two folded edges together. Worked from right to left, bring the needle out through one folded edge. Slip the needle through the fold of the opposite edge for about 6mm (¼in) and draw the needle and thread through. Continue in this manner.

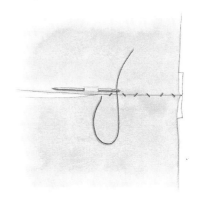

LOCKING STITCH

This stitch is used to hold the lining and interlining loosely to the main curtain.

1 Work from left to right with the lining/interlining folded back and nearest to you. Using a thread that matches exactly, secure the thread to the lining or interlining fold. With the needle vertical, make a small stitch by picking up a few threads from the main fabric and the lining/interlining, passing the needle point over the working thread, as shown. Draw the needle through, making sure you do not pull the stitch too tight.

2 Make a second stitch 10-15cm (4-6in) to the right, as described above. Continue making stitches spaced 10-15cm (4-6in) apart.

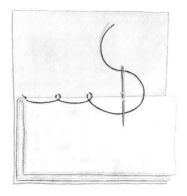

WHIPSTITCH

This is used to hold two finished edges together. Working from right to left, insert the needle at a right

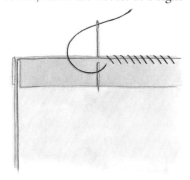

angle to the edge and picking up just a few threads from the fabric on both edges, draw the needle and thread through. Move a little way to the left and repeat until the two edges are joined.

HERRINGBONE STITCH

Used to hold hems firmly in place, this stitch is worked from left to right with the hem fold facing you and the needle pointing to the left.

1 Fasten the thread and bring the needle up through the hem 3mm (⅛in) in from the edge.

2 Move the needle up and to the right, picking up two threads from the single layer of fabric. Pull the needle through. Move the needle down to the right, and take another tiny stitch in the hem. Continue keeping all the stitches the same size.

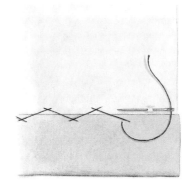

SLIP HEMMING

This stitch is used to hold a folded edge to a flat surface. It is almost invisible on the right side and is worked from right to left with the needle almost parallel to the stitching line.

Bring the needle out of the fold of the fabric and pick up two threads from the fabric directly below. Take the needle back into the folded edge and run the needle inside the

fold for approximately 1cm (⅜in). Bring the needle out and draw the thread through. Continue in the same manner, making sure the stitches are not pulled too tightly, or the fabric will look puckered on the right side.

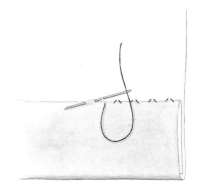

RUNNING STITCH

Pass the needle over and under the fabric, making the upper stitches of equal length. The understitches should also be of equal length, but at least half the size of the upper stitches.

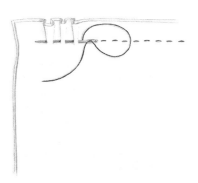

OVERCAST STITCH

This is the customary hand stitch for finishing raw edges of fabric to prevent them from fraying. In general, the more the fabric frays, the deeper and closer together the stitches should be worked. Working from either direction, take diagonal stitches over the edge, spacing them an even distance apart at a uniform depth.

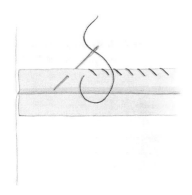

Embroidery stitches

BACKSTITCH

Start by bringing the needle up through to the right side of the fabric and make a short stitch backwards towards the right along the working line of the design. Take a long stitch to the left along the working line, on the reverse of the fabric and bring the needle out to the right side of the fabric. Take another short stitch back to the right and insert the needle down through the fabric at the start of the last short stitch. Now simply repeat the process for the desired length.

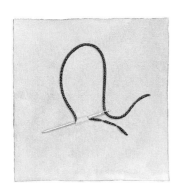

BLANKET STITCH

Work from left to right, with the point of the needle and working edge towards you. Bring the needle out by the edge. For the first stitch, insert the needle down through the fabric approx 3mm (⅛in) up from the edge and across to the right

(this gives a small stitch; increase the distance for larger stitches). Take a straight downwards stitch, bringing the needle back out at the edge and keeping the thread under the needle point. Draw the needle and thread through to form a looped stitch at the edge. Continue in the same way, spacing stitches evenly.

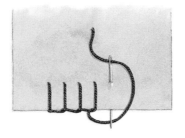

CHAIN STITCH

Bring the thread through from the back of the fabric to the front and hold down the thread with the thumb. Insert the needle back through the fabric where it emerged and make a small stitch bringing the needle through to the right side. Pull needle through, keeping the working thread under the point of the needle, to form a looped stitch on the right side. Repeat, taking the point of the needle down into the loop of the previous stitch and continue along the line of the design.

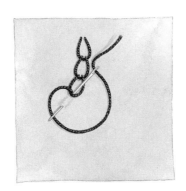

SATIN STITCH

This is a freestyle embroidery stitch, which is worked over a design that has been traced, printed or transferred on to a fabric.

Work straight stitches closely together across the shape on your design, as shown in the diagram. If desired, to give a raised effect, running stitch or chain stitch can be worked first over the shape to form a padding. The most important thing is to try to keep a good shape to your edge, and don't make the stitches too long, otherwise they are liable to catch on something and pull out of position.

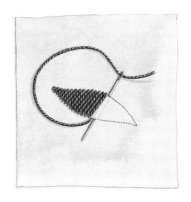

glossary of terms

Appliqué The technique of stitching fabric shapes on to a background to create a design. It can be applied either by hand or machine with a decorative embroidery stitch, such as buttonhole, or satin stitch.

Backstitch See Technique know-how, page 93.

Basting Also known as tacking in Great Britain. This is a means of holding two fabric layers together temporarily with large hand stitches.

Batting Also known as wadding in the UK, batting is the middle layer, or padding in a quilt or cushion. It can be made of cotton, wool or synthetic fibres, and can be bought in sheets, or as loose stuffing.

Bias The diagonal grain of a fabric. This is the direction which has the most give or stretch, making it ideal for bindings, especially on curved edges.

Binding A strip of fabric, either straight-grain or bias (cut on the diagonal). Can be used to bind edges, or for piping.

Blanket stitch See Technique know-how, page 93.

Bump A soft, blanket-like layer used as interlining.

Calico A raw unbleached cotton with a plain weave.

Canvas Heavy strong, plain weave fabric usually made from cotton, but sometimes from artificial fibres or blends. Used for blinds and chair seat covers.

Chalk pencils Available in various colours, they are used for marking lines, or spots on fabric. Some pencils have a brush attached, although marks are easily removed.

Ditch quilting Also known as quilting-in-the-ditch or stitch-in-the-ditch. The quilting stitches are worked along the actual seam lines, to give a pieced quilt texture. This is a particularly good technique for beginners as the stitches cannot be seen – only their effect.

Dressmakers' carbon paper Sometimes sold as tracing paper. Available in a number of colours, for light or dark fabric. It can be used with pencils, or a tracing wheel to transfer a design on to fabric.

Elasticised shirring See Technique know-how, page 90.

Embroidery hoop Consists of two wooden circular or oval rings with a screw adjuster on the outer ring. It stabilises the fabric, helping to create an even tension.

Face-fixed Fixing curtains outside the window recess.

Fade away marker pen A special felt tip pen for making marks on the right side of fabric as a guide for stitching. The marks gradually fade away without the use of water.

Finished drop The length of the finished curtain when hung.

Finished width The measurement from side edge to side edge once the curtain is gathered up.

Flat fell seams See Technique know-how, page 88.

French seams See Technique know-how, page 88.

Grain The direction in which the threads run in a woven fabric. In a vertical direction it is called the lengthwise grain, which has very little stretch. The horizontal direction, or crosswise grain is slightly stretchy, but diagonally the fabric has a lot of stretch. This grain is called the bias.

Herringbone stitch See Technique know-how, page 92.

Iron-on interfacing eg. Vilene/Pellon. A non-woven supporting material with adhesive that melts when ironed, making the interfacing adhere to the fabric.

Lapped seams See Technique know-how, page 89.

Leading edge Edge of the curtain at the centre when the curtains are closed. Or, on a single curtain, the edge that you draw across.

Locking stitches See Technique know-how, page 92.

Mitring See Technique know-how, page 90.

Overlock machine (or serger) This machine does not replace a conventional sewing machine, but compliments it. Overlocking is a quick way of finishing off seams and hem edges, as it cuts and neatens in one operation.

Paper-backed adhesive web eg. Bondaweb/Wonder-Under. Can be cut to shape and pressed to the wrong side of a fabric shape using a hot iron. Then the paper backing is peeled off. The fabric shape can then be placed on top of another, adhesive side down, and pressed again to fuse in place.

Patchwork The technique of stitching small pieces or patches of fabric together to create a larger piece of fabric, usually to form a pattern or design.

Pencil pleat heading A curtain heading formed with a tape which creates a row of densely-packed narrow pleats.

Pinking shears These cut with a zigzag fray-resistant edge. Excellent for finishing seams and raw edges on many types of fabric; also for creating decorative edges.

Pins Use good quality pins. Do not use thick, burred or rusted pins which will leave holes or marks. Long pins with glass or plastic heads are easier to use when pinning through thick fabrics.

Piping Fabric-covered piping cord used to emphasize the edges of cushions, tiebacks and other soft furnishings.

Quilting Traditionally done by hand with running stitches, but for speed a machine is usually used. The stitches are sewn through the top, padding and backing to hold the three layers together. Quilting stitches are usually worked in some form of design, but they can be random.

abbreviations

Recessed window A window set back into a wall. You can hang a blind or curtain inside it.

Running stitch See Technique know-how, page 92.

Satin stitch See Technique know-how, page 93.

Seam allowance The narrow strip of raw-edged fabric left after making a seam, to allow for fraying.

Selvedges Also known as selvages, these are the firmly-woven edges down each side of a fabric length. Selvedges should be trimmed off before cutting out your fabric, as they are more liable to shrink when the fabric is washed.

Slipstitch See Technique know-how, page 91.

Stitch-in-the-ditch See ditch quilting.

Tailor's chalk These are wedge-shaped pieces of chalk, available in several colours for marking on fabric.

Tear-away backing A non-woven material resembling parchment used underneath fabric to support it while embroidering by machine or hand.

Template A shape made from card or paper which is used as a pattern to mark outlines on fabric.

Warp These are the yarns running along the length of a fabric, parallel to the selvedges. They are usually stronger, and sometimes thicker than the threads running in the opposite direction.

Walking foot Also known as a quilting foot. This is a sewing machine foot with dual feed control. It is very helpful when quilting, as the fabric layers are fed evenly from the top and below, reducing the risk of slippage and puckering.

Weft These are the yarns running across the width of the fabric and interlocking with the warp yarns.

Whipstitch See Technique know-how, page 92.

The Kaffe Fassett Fabric collection

Stripes

NS	Narrow Stripe
PS	Pachrangi Stripe
ES	Exotic Stripe
AS	Alternate Stripe
BS	Broad Stripe
OS	Ombre Stripe
BWS	Blue and White Stripe
RS	Rowan Stripe

Checks

NC	Narrow Check
BC	Broad Check
EC	Exotic Check

Prints

GP 01	Roman Glass
GP 02	Damask
GP 03	Gazania
GP 07	Artichokes
GP 08	Forget-me-not Rose
GP 09	Chard
GP 11	Flower Lattice
GP 12	Floral Dance
GP 13	Chrysanthemum
GP 14	Dotty
GP 15	Bubbles

Print colour numbers

L	Leafy
J	Jewel
S	Stones
C	Circus
P	Pastel
R	Red
BW	Blue and White
PK	Pink
G	Gold
M	Magenta
O	Ochre
MV	Mauve
GRY	Grey
SB	Sky Blue
COB	Colbat
GRN	Green
PL	Plum
B	Blue
SG	Sea Green
TC	Terracotta
D	Driftwood
LV	Lavender
SU	Summer

Shot Cottons

SC 01	Ginger
SC 02	Cassis
SC 03	Prune
SC 04	Slate
SC 05	Opal
SC 07	Persimmon
SC 08	Raspberry
SC 09	Pomegranate
SC 10	Bittersweet
SC 11	Tangerine
SC 12	Chartreuse
SC 14	Lavender
SC 15	Denim Blue
SC 16	Mustard
SC 17	Sage
SC 18	Tobacco
SC 19	Lichen
SC 20	Smoky
SC 21	Pine
SC 22	Pewter
SC 23	Stone Grey
SC 24	Ecru
SC 25	Charcoal
SC 26	Duck Egg
SC 27	Grass
SC 28	Blush
SC 30	Custard
SC 31	Mushroom
SC 32	Rosy
SC 33	Water Melon
SC 34	Lemon
SC 35	Sunshine
SC 36	Lilac
SC 37	Coffee
SC 38	Biscuit
SC 39	Apple
SC 40	Cobalt
SC 41	Jade
SC 42	Rush
SC 43	Lime

The Kaffe Fassett Fabric Collection

The Kaffe Fassett fabrics are available at Rowan stockists in Europe and the Far East. In USA, Canada and Australia they are available through Westminster stockists and better fabric shops. Please call Rowan Tel: +44 (0) 1484 681881 for stockist details.

100% COTTON ■ **FABRIC WIDTH 114cm (45in)**   Please note: Due to printing, colours may not be true to life.

Shot Cotton

SC 01 Ginger	SC 02 Cassis	SC 03 Prune	SC 04 Slate	SC 05 Opal	SC 07 Persimmon
SC 08 Raspberry	SC 09 Pomegranate	SC 10 Bittersweet	SC 11 Tangerine	SC 12 Chartreuse	SC 14 Lavender
SC 15 Denim Blue	SC 16 Mustard	SC 17 Sage	SC 18 Tobacco	SC 19 Lichen	SC 20 Smoky
SC 21 Pine	SC 22 Pewter	SC 23 Stone Grey	SC 24 Ecru	SC 25 Charcoal	SC 26 Duck Egg
SC 27 Grass	SC 28 Blush	SC 30 Custard	SC 31 Mushroom	SC 32 Rosy	SC 33 Water Melon
SC 34 Lemon	SC 35 Sunshine	SC 36 Lilac	SC 37 Coffee	SC 38 Biscuit	SC 39 Apple

■ **WASH FABRIC BEFORE USE.**

Prewash all new fabrics before you begin to ensure that there will be no uneven shrinkage and no bleeding of colours in later laundering. Press the fabric whilst it is still damp to return crispness to it.

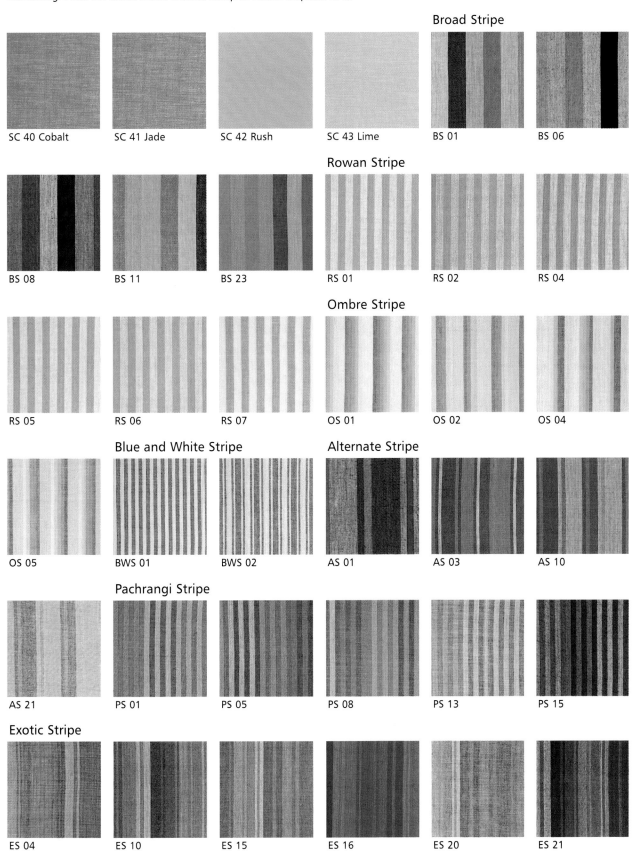

Broad Stripe

SC 40 Cobalt   SC 41 Jade   SC 42 Rush   SC 43 Lime   BS 01   BS 06

Rowan Stripe

BS 08   BS 11   BS 23   RS 01   RS 02   RS 04

Ombre Stripe

RS 05   RS 06   RS 07   OS 01   OS 02   OS 04

Blue and White Stripe   ## Alternate Stripe

OS 05   BWS 01   BWS 02   AS 01   AS 03   AS 10

Pachrangi Stripe

AS 21   PS 01   PS 05   PS 08   PS 13   PS 15

Exotic Stripe

ES 04   ES 10   ES 15   ES 16   ES 20   ES 21

The Kaffe Fassett Fabric Collection

Narrow Stripe

NS 01 NS 08 NS 09 NS 13 NS 16 NS 17

Broad Check   Narrow Check

BC 01 BC 02 BC 03 BC 04 NC 01 NC 02

Exotic Check

NC 03 NC 05 EC 01 EC 02 EC 03 EC 05

Roman Glass

GP 01-L GP 01-J GP 01-S GP 01-C GP 01-P GP 01-G

Damask

GP 01-BW GP 01-PK GP 01-R GP 02-L GP 02-J GP 02-P

Gazania

GP 03-L GP 03-J GP 03-S GP 03-C GP 03-P

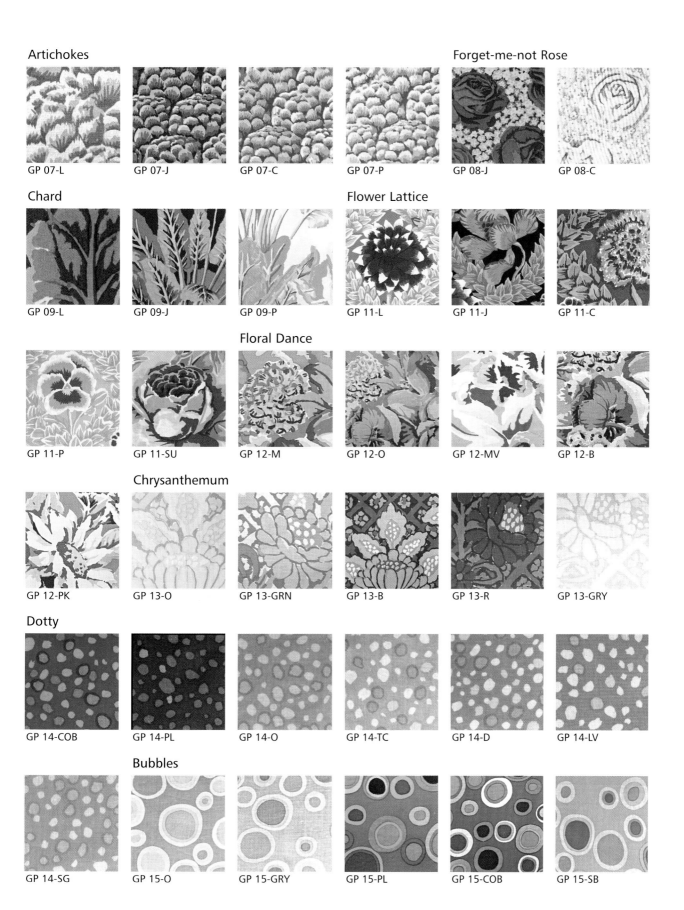

Artichokes

GP 07-L   GP 07-J   GP 07-C   GP 07-P

Forget-me-not Rose

GP 08-J   GP 08-C

Chard

GP 09-L   GP 09-J   GP 09-P

Flower Lattice

GP 11-L   GP 11-J   GP 11-C

Floral Dance

GP 11-P   GP 11-SU   GP 12-M   GP 12-O   GP 12-MV   GP 12-B

Chrysanthemum

GP 12-PK   GP 13-O   GP 13-GRN   GP 13-B   GP 13-R   GP 13-GRY

Dotty

GP 14-COB   GP 14-PL   GP 14-O   GP 14-TC   GP 14-D   GP 14-LV

Bubbles

GP 14-SG   GP 15-O   GP 15-GRY   GP 15-PL   GP 15-COB   GP 15-SB

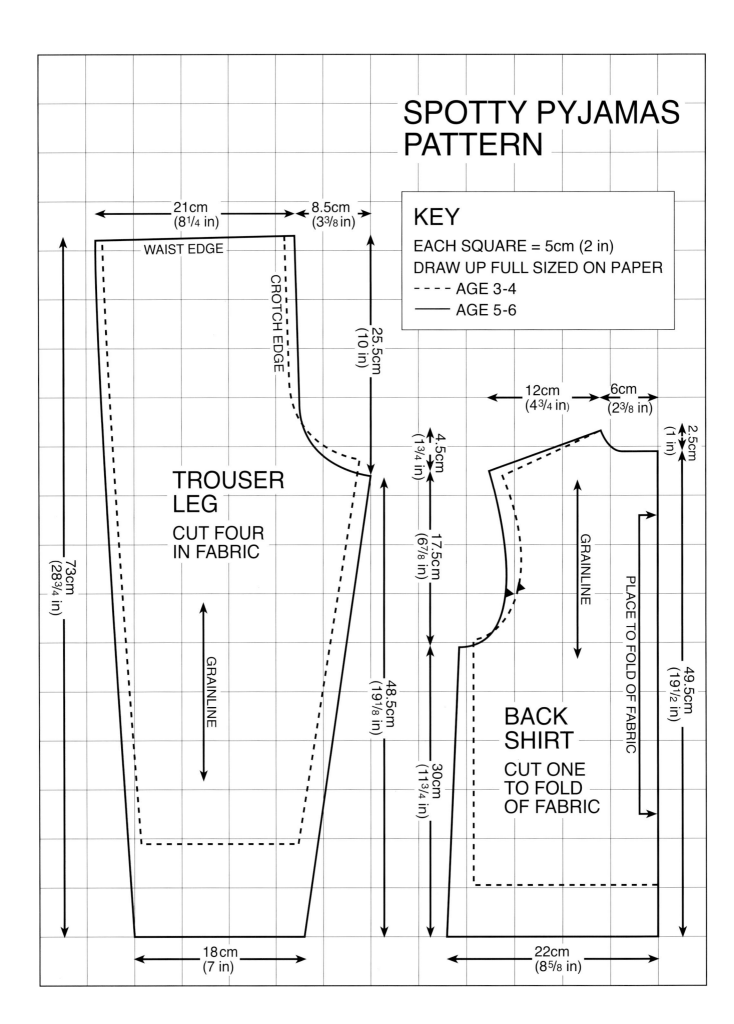

SPOTTY PYJAMAS PATTERN

KEY

EACH SQUARE = 5cm (2 in)
DRAW UP FULL SIZED ON PAPER
- - - - AGE 3-4
——— AGE 5-6

21cm (8¼ in)
8.5cm (3⅜ in)
WAIST EDGE
CROTCH EDGE
25.5cm (10 in)

TROUSER LEG
CUT FOUR IN FABRIC

GRAINLINE

73cm (28¾ in)

48.5cm (19⅛ in)

18cm (7 in)

12cm (4¾ in)
6cm (2⅜ in)
2.5cm (1 in)

4.5cm (1¾ in)
17.5cm (6⅞ in)

GRAINLINE

PLACE TO FOLD OF FABRIC

49.5cm (19½ in)

BACK SHIRT
CUT ONE TO FOLD OF FABRIC

30cm (11¾ in)

22cm (8⅝ in)

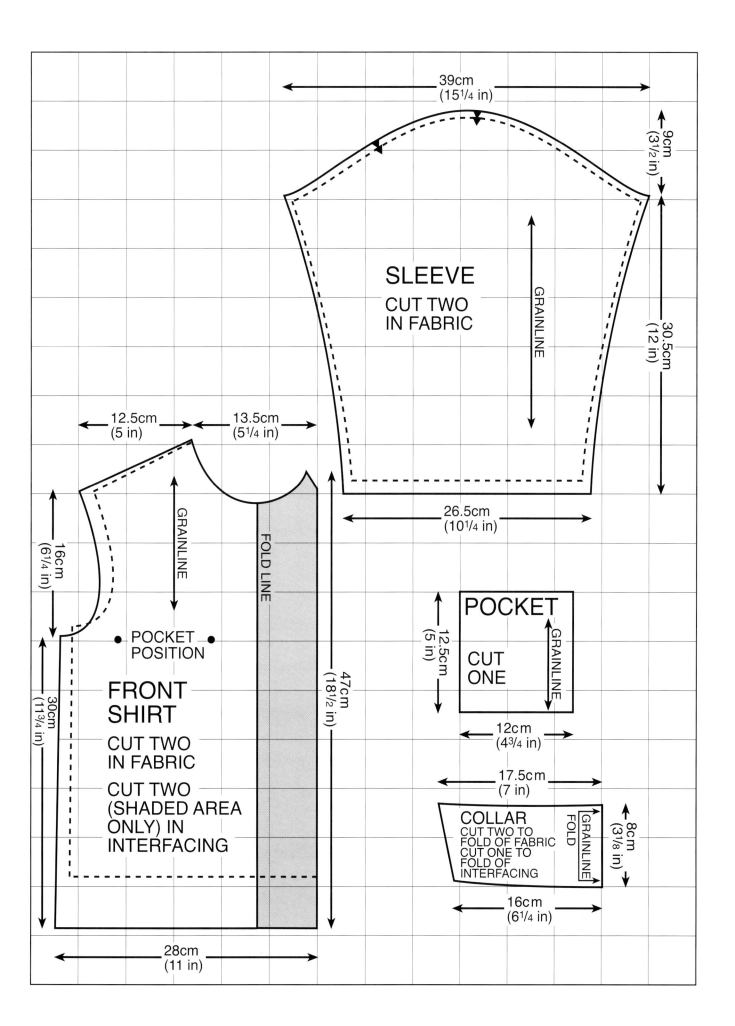

39cm
(15¼ in)

9cm
(3½ in)

30.5cm
(12 in)

SLEEVE
CUT TWO
IN FABRIC

GRAINLINE

26.5cm
(10¼ in)

12.5cm
(5 in)

13.5cm
(5¼ in)

GRAINLINE

FOLD LINE

16cm
(6¼ in)

POCKET
POSITION

47cm
(18½ in)

FRONT
SHIRT

CUT TWO
IN FABRIC

CUT TWO
(SHADED AREA
ONLY) IN
INTERFACING

30cm
(11¾ in)

28cm
(11 in)

POCKET

12.5cm
(5 in)

CUT
ONE

GRAINLINE

12cm
(4¾ in)

17.5cm
(7 in)

COLLAR
CUT TWO TO
FOLD OF FABRIC
CUT ONE TO
FOLD OF
INTERFACING

GRAINLINE
FOLD

8cm
(3⅛ in)

16cm
(6¼ in)

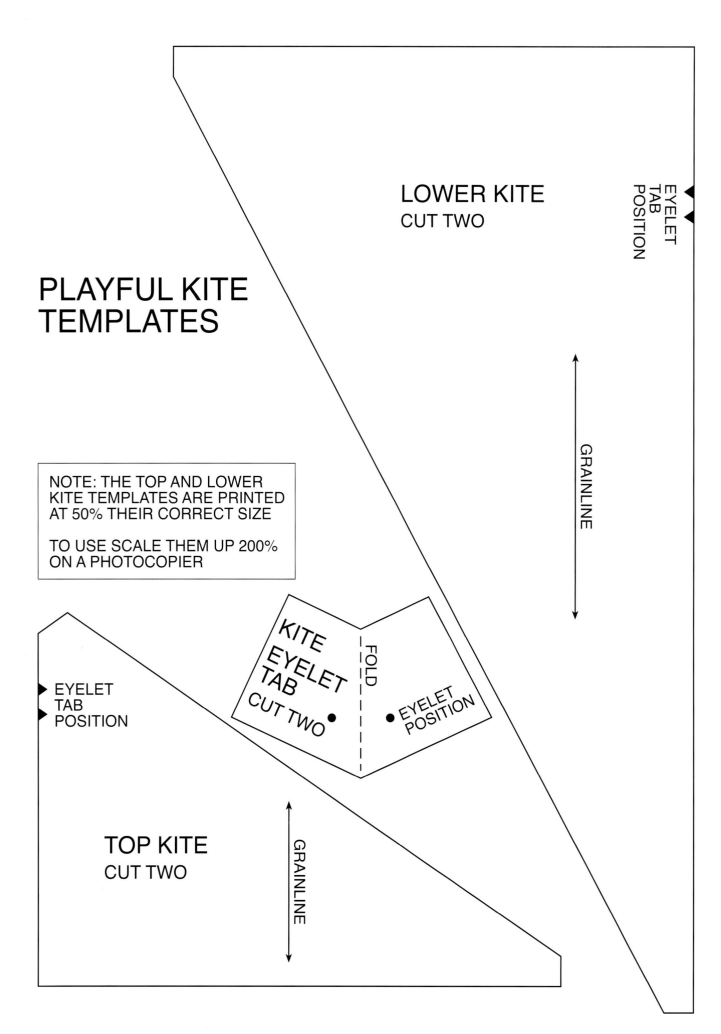

PLAYFUL KITE TEMPLATES

LOWER KITE
CUT TWO

EYELET TAB POSITION

GRAINLINE

NOTE: THE TOP AND LOWER KITE TEMPLATES ARE PRINTED AT 50% THEIR CORRECT SIZE

TO USE SCALE THEM UP 200% ON A PHOTOCOPIER

KITE EYELET TAB CUT TWO

FOLD

EYELET POSITION

EYELET TAB POSITION

TOP KITE
CUT TWO

GRAINLINE

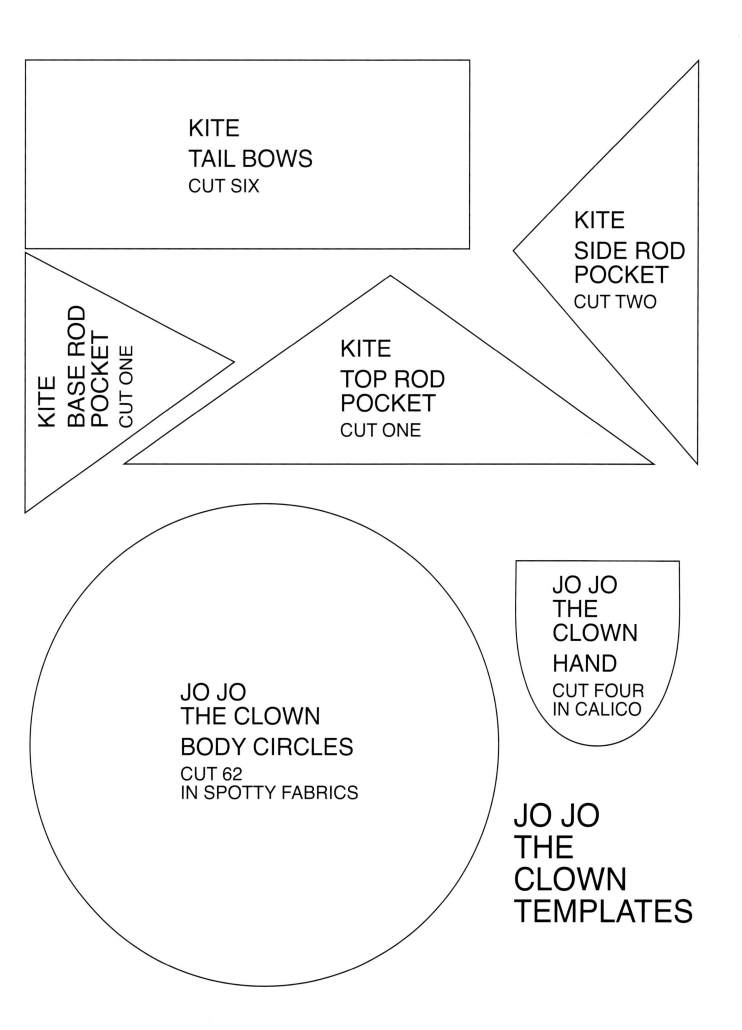

KITE
TAIL BOWS
CUT SIX

KITE
SIDE ROD
POCKET
CUT TWO

KITE
BASE ROD
POCKET CUT ONE

KITE
TOP ROD
POCKET
CUT ONE

JO JO
THE CLOWN
BODY CIRCLES
CUT 62
IN SPOTTY FABRICS

JO JO
THE
CLOWN
HAND
CUT FOUR
IN CALICO

JO JO
THE
CLOWN
TEMPLATES

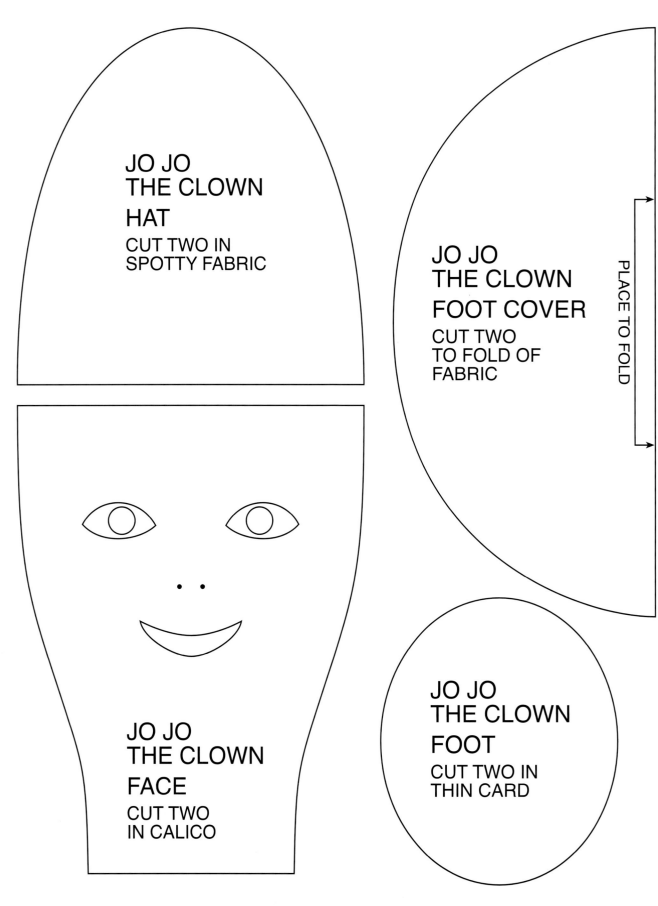

JO JO
THE CLOWN
HAT
CUT TWO IN
SPOTTY FABRIC

JO JO
THE CLOWN
FOOT COVER
CUT TWO
TO FOLD OF
FABRIC

PLACE TO FOLD

JO JO
THE CLOWN
FACE
CUT TWO
IN CALICO

JO JO
THE CLOWN
FOOT
CUT TWO IN
THIN CARD

JO JO THE CLOWN TEMPLATES

BED QUILT
QUILTING DIAGRAM

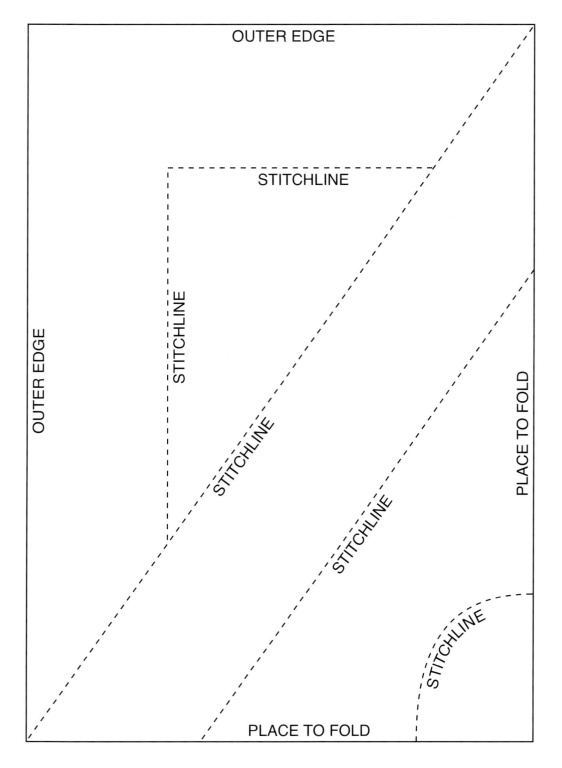

NOTE: THIS DIAGRAM IS 25% OF ACTUAL QUILT SIZE

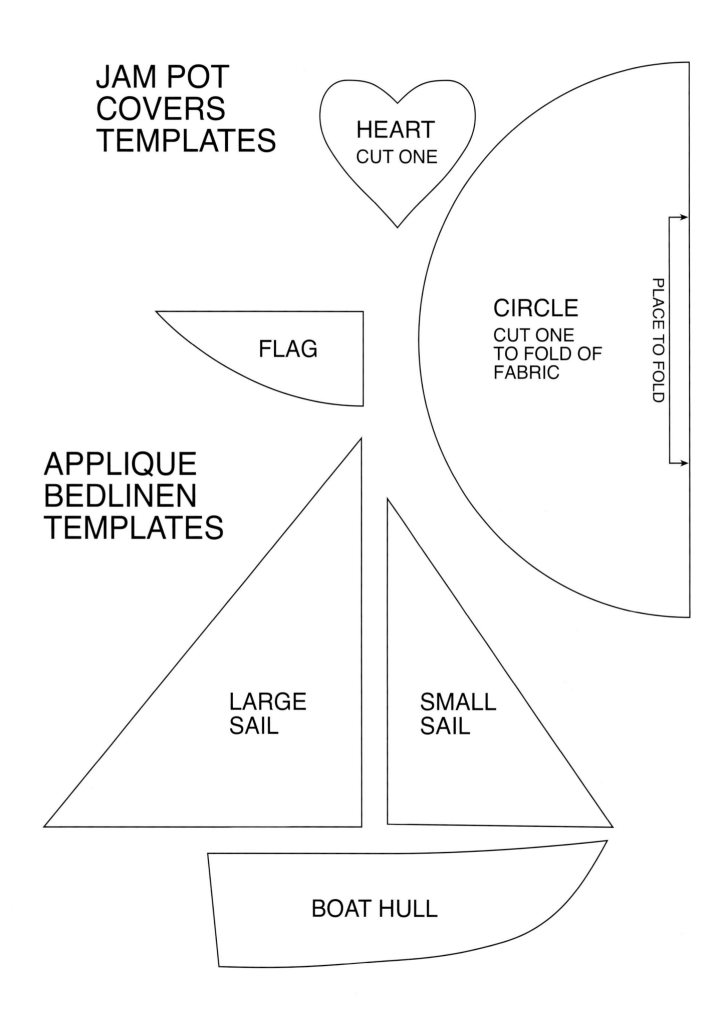

JAM POT
COVERS
TEMPLATES

HEART
CUT ONE

CIRCLE
CUT ONE
TO FOLD OF
FABRIC

PLACE TO FOLD

FLAG

APPLIQUE
BEDLINEN
TEMPLATES

LARGE
SAIL

SMALL
SAIL

BOAT HULL

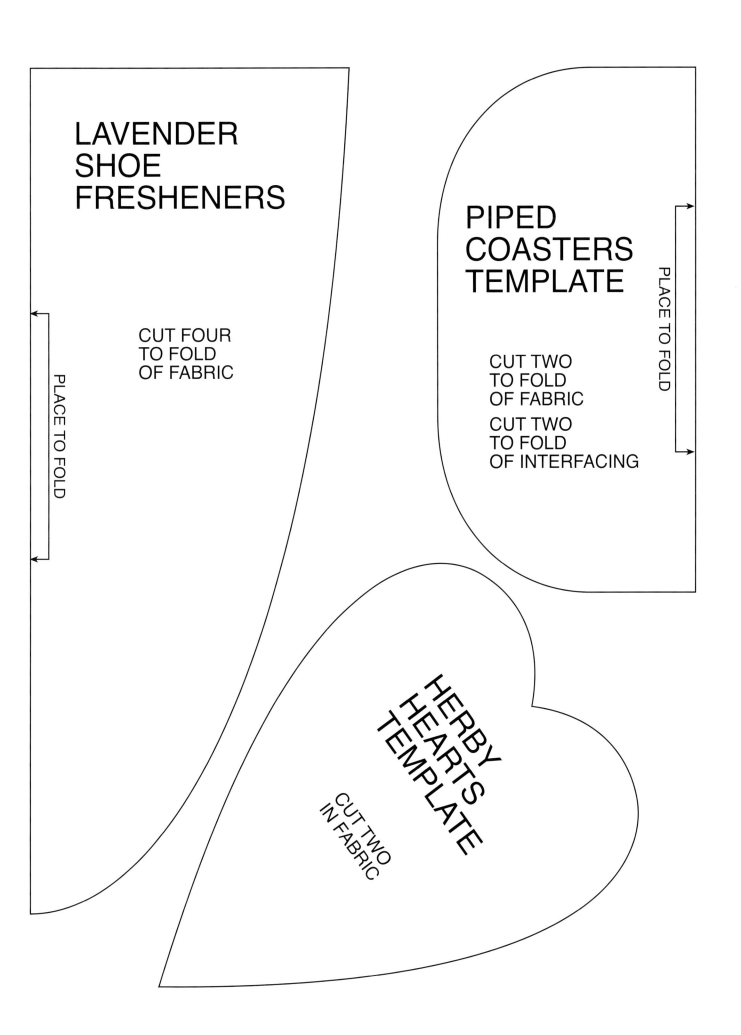

LAVENDER
SHOE
FRESHENERS

CUT FOUR
TO FOLD
OF FABRIC

PLACE TO FOLD

PIPED
COASTERS
TEMPLATE

PLACE TO FOLD

CUT TWO
TO FOLD
OF FABRIC

CUT TWO
TO FOLD
OF INTERFACING

HERBY
HEARTS
TEMPLATE

CUT TWO
IN FABRIC

HARLEQUIN
TEA COSY
TEMPLATES

PATCHWORK
SQUARE
TEMPLATE

NOTE: THE TEA COSY
TEMPLATE IS PRINTED
AT 50% ITS CORRECT SIZE

TO USE SCALE IT UP 200%
ON A PHOTOCOPIER

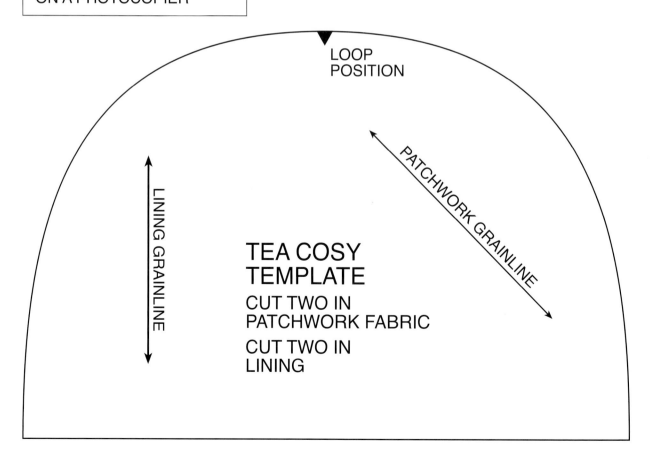

LOOP
POSITION

LINING GRAINLINE

PATCHWORK GRAINLINE

TEA COSY
TEMPLATE

CUT TWO IN
PATCHWORK FABRIC

CUT TWO IN
LINING

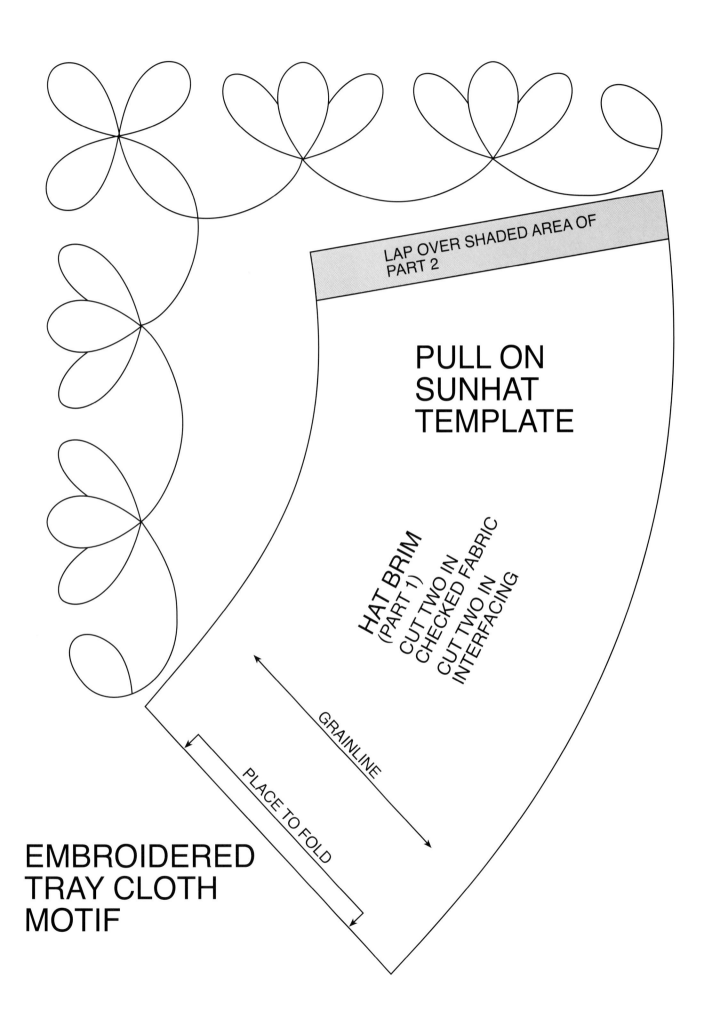

LAP OVER SHADED AREA OF
PART 2

PULL ON
SUNHAT
TEMPLATE

HAT BRIM
(PART 1)
CUT TWO IN
CHECKED FABRIC
CUT TWO IN
INTERFACING

GRAINLINE

PLACE TO FOLD

EMBROIDERED
TRAY CLOTH
MOTIF

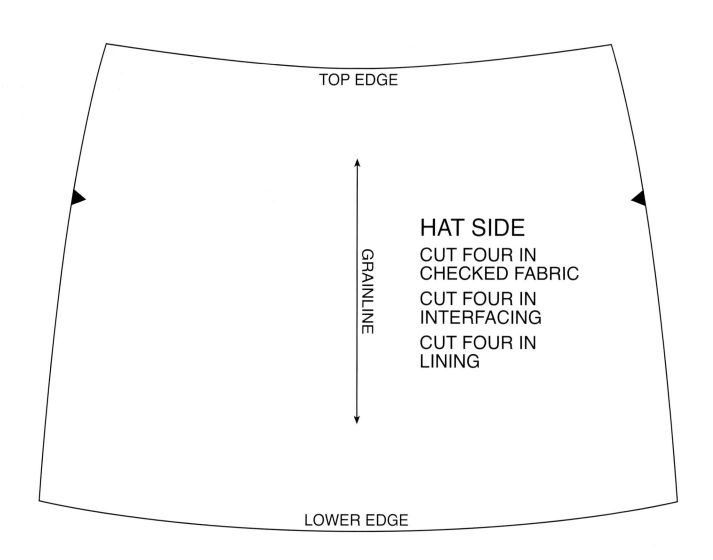

TOP EDGE

GRAINLINE

HAT SIDE

CUT FOUR IN
CHECKED FABRIC

CUT FOUR IN
INTERFACING

CUT FOUR IN
LINING

LOWER EDGE

PULL ON SUN HAT TEMPLATES

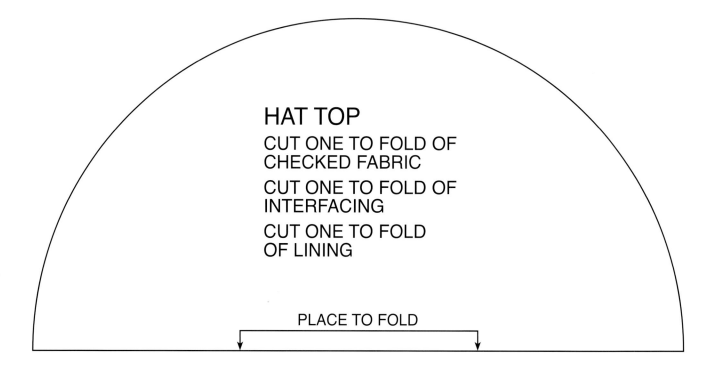

HAT TOP

CUT ONE TO FOLD OF
CHECKED FABRIC

CUT ONE TO FOLD OF
INTERFACING

CUT ONE TO FOLD
OF LINING

PLACE TO FOLD

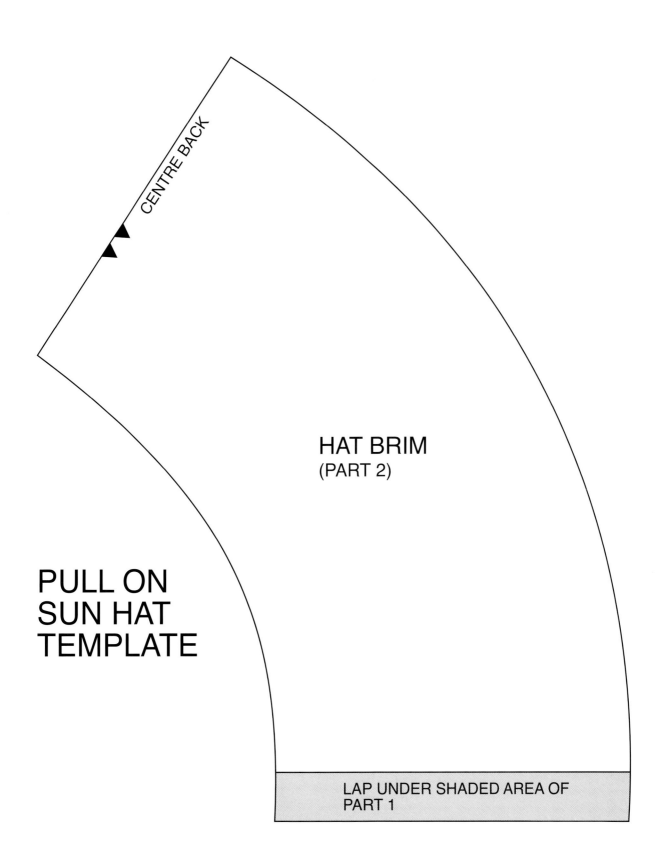

CENTRE BACK

HAT BRIM
(PART 2)

PULL ON
SUN HAT
TEMPLATE

LAP UNDER SHADED AREA OF
PART 1

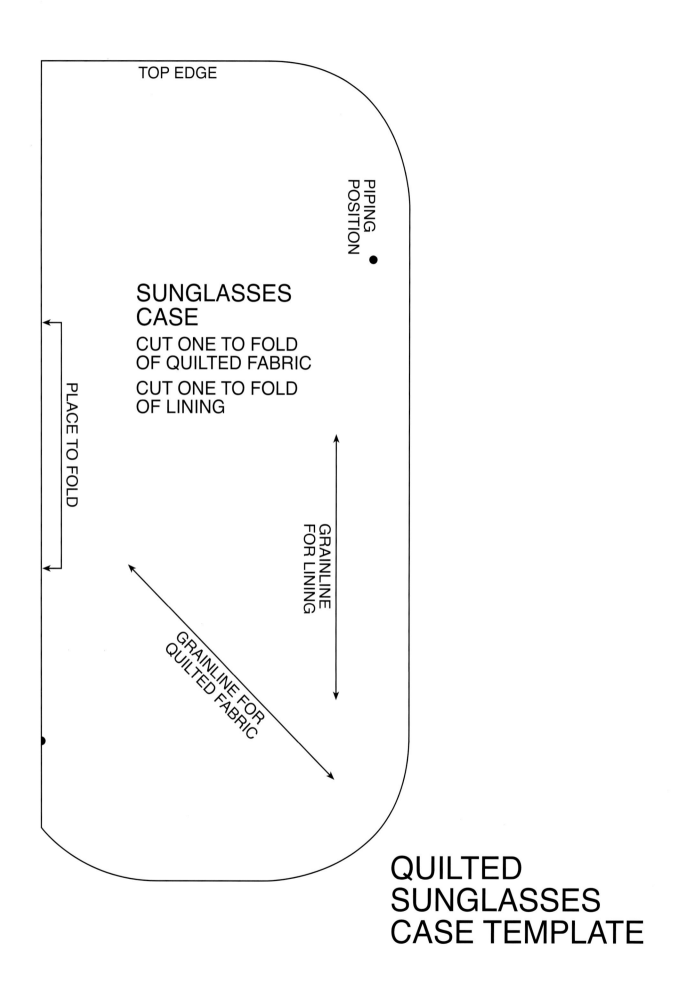

TOP EDGE

PIPING
POSITION

SUNGLASSES
CASE

CUT ONE TO FOLD
OF QUILTED FABRIC

CUT ONE TO FOLD
OF LINING

PLACE TO FOLD

GRAINLINE
FOR LINING

GRAINLINE FOR
QUILTED FABRIC

QUILTED
SUNGLASSES
CASE TEMPLATE

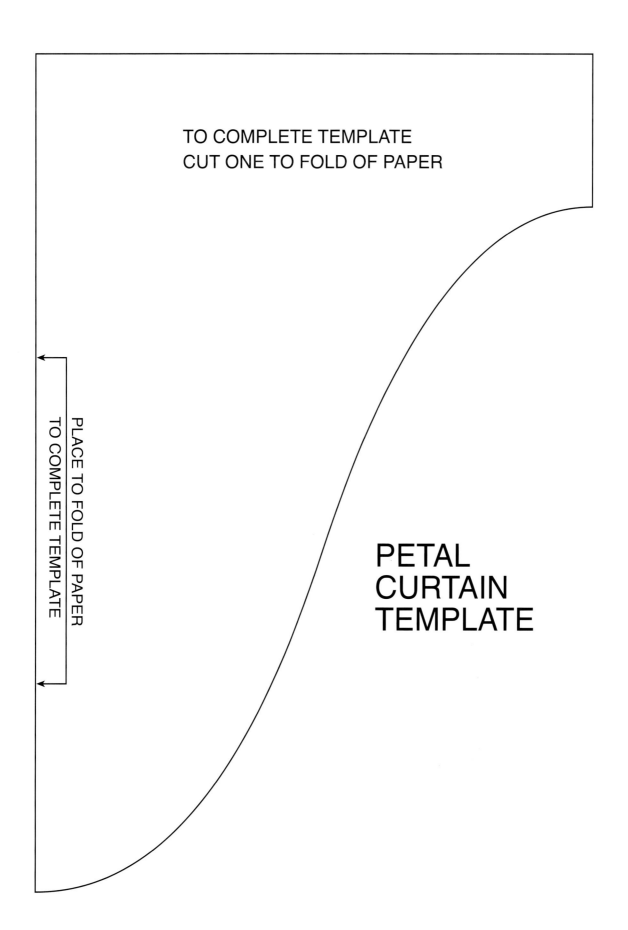

TO COMPLETE TEMPLATE
CUT ONE TO FOLD OF PAPER

PLACE TO FOLD OF PAPER
TO COMPLETE TEMPLATE

PETAL
CURTAIN
TEMPLATE

Other Rowan titles available

**Patchwork and Quilting
Book Number One
£7.50**

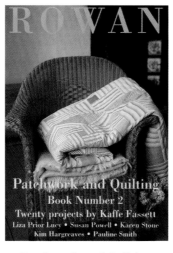

**Patchwork and Quilting
Book Number Two
£9.95**

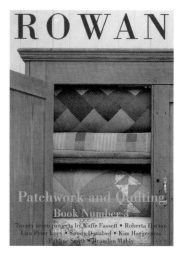

**Patchwork and Quilting
Book Number Three
£10.95**

**Patchwork and Quilting
Book Number Four
£12.95**

**Rowan Living
Book One
£12.95**

R O W A N

Green Mill, Holmfirth, West Yorkshire, England
Tel: +44 (0) 1484 681881   Fax: +44 (0) 1484 687920   Internet: www.knitrowan.com
Email: Mail@knitrowan.com

index

Author's acknowledgements

We would like to thank all those who have given their time and expertise to make this book possible. Especially Mark Scott for his enthusiasm and skill in giving us such beautiful pictures, and to Nicky at Downes Design for turning our ideas into the finished book.

In addition we would like to thank Julia and Chris Cowper for letting us photograph in their seaside house. Thanks too, to Gaye Hawkins and Beryl Miller who helped us make the projects. To Breeze, Dorma, Fired Earth, Quintessential, Summerhouse, Sandra Jane and The Warehouse for loaning us props so generously, and to Husqvarna Viking for providing us with a fabulous sewing machine. And not forgetting our gorgeous models, Jody and Ebony.

All Drima and Sylko machine threads, Anchor embroidery threads, and Prym sewing aids, distributed in UK by Coats Crafts UK, P.O Box 22, Lingfield House, Lingfield Point, McMullen Road, Darlington, Co. Durham, DL1 1YQ. Consumer helpline: 01325 394237. Anchor embroidery thread and Coats sewing threads, distributed in the USA by Coats & Clark, 4135 South Stream Blvd, Charlotte, North Carolina 28217. Tel: 704 329 5016. Fax: 704 329 5027. Prym products distributed in the USA by Prym-Dritz Corp, 950 Brisack Road, Spartanburg, SC 29303. Tel: +1 864 576 5050, Fax: +1 864 587 3353, e-mail: pdmar@teleplex.net

Breeze 01223 354403; Dorma 0161 251 4400; Fired Earth 01295 812088; Husqvarna Viking 01934 744533 www.husqvarnaviking.com; Quintessential 01223 525717; Summerhouse 01223 264 441; Sandra Jane 01223 300613; The Warehouse 01328 738634